For many years a disciple of Naina Devi, ... performer of the delicate style of thumri–dadra singing. She studied khayal under the late Professor B.N. Datta and thereafter under Pandit Mani Prasad of the Kirana gharana. She continued her intensive training in thumri under Shanti Hiranand and Girija Devi.

A recipient of fellowships from the Ford Foundation, and the Department of Culture, Government of India, she has written extensively on music and the performing arts. She has been visiting professor at the School of Arts and Aesthetics, Jawaharlal Nehru University, Delhi, and visiting fellow at the Centre for Advanced Study, Jadavpur University, Kolkata.

Vidya Rao holds a master's degree in sociology from the Delhi School of Economics, Delhi University, has worked with several research organizations and is currently an editorial consultant with Orient Blackswan publishers.

Heart to Heart

Remembering Naina Devi

VIDYA RAO

HarperCollins *Publishers* India
a joint venture with

New Delhi

First published in India in 2011 by
HarperCollins *Publishers* India
a joint venture with
The India Today Group

Copyright © Vidya Rao 2011
Photographs courtesy Rena Ripjit Singh

ISBN: 978-93-5029-147-4

2 4 6 8 10 9 7 5 3 1

Vidya Rao asserts the moral right to be identified
as the author of this book.

HarperCollins *Publishers*
A-53, Sector 57, NOIDA, Uttar Pradesh – 201301, India
77-85 Fulham Palace Road, London W6 8JB, United Kingdom
Hazelton Lanes, 55 Avenue Road, Suite 2900, Toronto, Ontario M5R 3L2
and 1995 Markham Road, Scarborough, Ontario M1B 5M8, Canada
25 Ryde Road, Pymble, Sydney, NSW 2073, Australia
31 View Road, Glenfield, Auckland 10, New Zealand
10 East 53rd Street, New York NY 10022, USA

Typeset in 10/13 Minion Pro
Jojy Philip New Delhi 110 015

Printed and bound at
Thomson Press (India) Ltd.

To my mother,
for my childhood of songs and stories
and to my daughter,
for letting me relive that childhood with her.

Acknowledgements

My deepest gratitude to the memory of Nainaji for her presence in my life.

My deepest gratitude also to my present gurus—Vidushi Shanti Hiranand, Vidushi Girija Devi, Pandit Mani Prasad, and also to the late Professor B.N. Datta for the gift of their guidance.

But for Professor Veena Das's suggestion that I write this, and her many comments on its first draft, I may never have begun this work. Rajni Palriwala and Nandini Rao read the earlier drafts. I am grateful to them all.

Rena Singh, Naina Devi's daughter, encouraged me in this venture as in everything, shared her memories with me and provided the photographs. Her encouragement has meant the world to me.

My family and my friends—nothing would be possible without their love, encouragement and support.

This book is part of the work I have been able to do with the help of grants from the Ford Foundation and the Department of Culture, Government of India. I thank these organizations for their support, and especially Shri Ashok Vajpeyi, Shri Anmol Vellani and Dr Mary Zurbuchen.

The initial draft of this book was written at the library

of the India International Centre. I am grateful to Dr Kaul, Ms Sushma Zutshi and the staff of the library for that most peaceful space, so conducive to work.

Abridged and edited excerpts of some chapters appeared in *Economic Times, Hindustan Times, India Magazine* and in a booklet produced by the Naina Devi Foundation. I thank these publications and organizations and especially Sadanand Menon and Kai Friese for their interest in and support of my work.

Seema Sagar helped me with keying in a manuscript that was in bits and pieces. Thank you, Seema.

V.K. Karthika of HarperCollins has gently but firmly insisted on my completing the book and competently taken charge thereafter. Minakshi Thakur's and Debika Roy Choudhry's queries helped me clarify my own thoughts. Shantanu Ray Chaudhuri has suffered the nitty-gritty of turning the manuscript into a book. Many thanks to them all.

Sufi, my cat, keeps me company in everything I do; I am sure we have been friends in other lives as well.

My son-in-law, Satyadeep guides me through the impenetrable mysteries of the computer, and generally looks after me as if he were my own son.

Nandini, the most wonderful sister a woman could have, helps me long distance with computer-related problems and everything else.

Above all, gratitude to my beloved daughter, Aditi, life's sweetest gift, for more than I can ever say.

1

Learning to Remember

It is nearly eighteen years since Naina Devi passed away. It has taken me all this time to come to terms with her passing, and to be able to place in perspective the years I spent with her. There are some wounds that, even with the passage of time, never quite heal. I realize this, today, as I pick up this half-written and then abandoned manuscript, and attempt to write this last (or first) chapter. Memories of Nainaji come flooding back and overwhelm me with their intensity. Eighteen years is a long time, and yet, it seems just yesterday that I wept like a child as her body was taken away on that last journey. In these years after her passing, I have learned, and am still learning, to absorb and incorporate the experiences of those years—all that she taught me, all that I tried to learn, all that happened. As I read through the chapters already written, and as I write this one, I am reliving the last two years of Naina Devi's life—seeing again her slow and reluctant decline into illness, and finally, into the irrevocability of death.

The loss of a guru is never easy. Gurus are parent-like figures, often more than parents to the shagird. Losing a guru is having to deal with a sense of being abandoned, orphaned. It is also to begin to try and understand why it is that one embarked on this journey and this relationship at all.

I had been Naina Devi's constant companion for all the years I was her student, and more so, through the last phase of her life. She had been ill for a period of about two years. A stroke, the second in fairly quick succession, had made her extremely fragile and ill. It was an illness that she spiritedly refused to acknowledge, but that nevertheless asserted its presence, and to which, finally, she had to succumb. But the end, when it came, was peaceful. Now I remember those days, and relive the hours spent in the hospital, waiting and praying. What were we praying for? What hope could there be? Later Nainaji's daughter, Rena Singh, was to tell me, 'I prayed for her release, for peace for her body and soul.'

I became Nainaji's shishya in the summer of 1986. I believe this was in answer to a deep desire to steep myself in the form of thumri. It was the singer and her student, Shubha Mudgal, who acted as the catalyst, encouraging me to overcome my hesitation and approach Naina Devi. I am deeply grateful to Shubha for this. I was fortunate, too, that soon after this, a generous fellowship for research on thumri released me from the need to work for my daily bread. I was thus able to spend almost all my waking hours with Nainaji, imbibing both her music and her being. This was my life until her passing in 1993.

I began writing this book well before Naina Devi died. It started as an attempt to write about the life of this extraordinary woman. I was trying to understand how women speak about themselves and their lives, and how they are heard, how they see (or do not see) themselves as embedded within the history of their times. I was interested in memory and history and story, and how a woman might recall her life, and how she might tell the events of her life to weave a story-like narrative. I was fortunate, too, that Professor Veena Das, my teacher from the Delhi School of Economics, suggested I write this.

Naina Devi saw a first draft of this book before she died. And then after her death, both the book and I went through several adventures. Dealing with the nitty-gritty of life in a big city, I put the manuscript away for many years, until now. I am glad I did so. I realize I needed some distance from Nainaji and the life I shared with her, and indeed from what I had written. Rereading and rewriting now have meant remembering and experiencing again those days, Nainaji's presence, and also the woman I once was.

When musicians use the phrase 'yaad karna', they mean both to commit to memory, and also to learn. Writing this book has meant remembering all that she told me. Remembering has meant reconnecting, but also learning, understanding, assimilating and moving on—a process of growth.

I have had the good fortune to learn and continue to receive taleem from other gurus equally dear to me. They include the late Professor B.N. Datta, Pandit Mani Prasad, Vidushi Shanti Hiranand and Vidushi Girija Devi. But it was with Nainaji and no one else that I was able to spend the maximum time. Part of this time was spent learning music, but part of it was time when we were able to just talk. Nainaji shared her experiences with me, listened to mine. With Nainaji, music and life both became teachings; from her I learned both music and how to live.

People reveal themselves differently to different people, and even reveal different aspects at different times. Also, each person sees and hears that revealing differently. As long as a person is alive, the process of telling a life is with the one who lives it (discounting the intrusions of modern media!). After her/his death, however, the story of a person's life becomes available to others for interpretation, invention and reinvention, even appropriation. In writing this book, I have tried to maintain the very fine line between subjectivity and appropriation.

A person is known subjectively through the prism of one's own being. This is the way Naina Devi revealed herself to me and this is the way I heard her. And finally, this is the way I have remembered and learned. This is the way she lives on in my memory and in my music.

2

Patterning a Life

This story can only be written as I have heard and experienced it, in snatches, as a footnote attached to a bandish she is teaching me, as an example bringing out some hidden facet of a musical phrase. The beginning, I believe, is a good place to start—but where is the beginning? Perhaps I should start where it all began for me, from the point at which I entered this life.

It is a warm evening in June 1986. I have gone to ask Naina Devi, plucking up all my courage to do so, if she will accept me as her shagird and teach me thumri. I am afraid she will refuse, but to my surprise and great joy, she agrees so simply, so easily, that I am left speechless. Later I will learn that she is always like this. The quality of her chosen form, that her mentor Rasoolan Bai once described as sahuliyat—this quality of ease and grace permeates her being.

I should first introduce her. A small, slight woman with delicate features, her hair remarkably free of grey, she is sprightly, active and cheerful. Naina Devi.

She was born Nilina Sen in Calcutta on 27 September 1917. Daughter of Saral Chandra Sen and his wife Nirmala

(Nellie), granddaughter of Brahmananda Keshub Chandra Sen, an important leader of the Brahmo Samaj, Brahmo ideology, social reform and nationalist fervour dominated the environment in which she grew up. When I met her, these influences were still perceptible in her own thinking along with many other influences that she had absorbed.

Naina Devi is remembered as one of India's most important singers. During her lifetime, she was also known and is still remembered as a generous patron of musicians, and one who was a source of support to old and ailing artistes. Her chosen form was the delicate purab ang thumri of Banaras, and she was acknowledged by fellow musicians as one of the last true voices of this style. She was a veritable storehouse of traditional thumris and dadras, and her vast repertoire also included forms like chaiti, kajri, jhoola and barahmasa which are derived from folk music.

Thumri is one of the three major forms included today in the corpus of north Indian art music. The thumri of Banaras draws heavily on the folk music of the purab region (eastern UP and Bihar). But along with the rhythmic, folksy airs of these folk-music-derived forms, Banaras also gives us the expansive and introspective bol banao ki thumri.

Thumri is characterized by fluid movements—the glides of meend and soot, the quick twists of murkis, the short sharp spirals of tappa-style tans, and the heart-rending cry of pukar, but above all, its purity of swar. It differs from the more frequently heard khayal in its emphasis on the delineation of bol: in thumri the words of the bandish, the composition, are fleshed out and savoured. They receive the same detailed treatment as swar does. And it is characterized too by its emphasis on bhav or expression of emotion. Significantly, it was earlier sung primarily, though not only, by courtesans, to entertain elite male patrons. Writing about this form, Nainaji has explained how many have

> ... scoffed at this style of singing. Thumri is termed as light classical music. In actuality, it is the essence of dhrupad and khayal.... It is therefore not possible for a student to learn thumri without serious training.... Thumri is expressive and emotive music, which is steeped in shringar rasa.... Shringar is the king of the navrasas and covers the entire gamut of expression of human experience from the sensuous to the sublime....Great stress is laid on bol banana or conveying musically the meaning of a word in different ways with different connotations. The lyrics revolve around episodes from the lives of Radha and Krishna, or a lover and his beloved. This concept is known as madhurya bhakti and is symbolic of the yearning of the human soul to unite with the Universal Soul.... Thumri singing is extremely difficult and requires a sense of restraint and discrimination, combined with a perfect control of the voice. It can be likened to the making of a bouquet of flowers where the blending of colours, the choice of flowers and decorative leaves are borne in mind.

Thumri is a style of singing that is now almost lost to us, notwithstanding the efforts of people like Nainaji to keep it alive. Erotic and sensuous, today this style runs the risk of finding a platform and respectability either by thoroughly sanitizing itself, or alternatively, of miring itself in an excessively sensual or sentimental expression. Its true voice negotiates the tricky space between these two extremes. 'Thumri is about love,' Nainaji would often say. 'If the singer doesn't experience and express emotion, it ceases to be thumri. You must be able to communicate the mood of the bandish.'

How did she, a woman from a bhadralok family of Bengal, come to find her voice in this style of music that was sung by tawaifs or courtesans in the darbars of the Nawabs of Awadh and, till as late as the 1940s, continued to flourish in the courts of north India and in the festivals and mehfils of Banaras? It is a fascinating story, one that illustrates many of the issues that surfaced in the late nineteenth and early twentieth centuries—social reform, the changing position of women, changes in the world of music, in the status of performers, especially women performers, patronage, and the perception of the place of music in our lives.

Listening, learning, participating, and now writing, I recognize that there is no one story after all. Each strand of the fabric that is a life is a complete story, and each such story bears some resemblance to all other strands that make up the unending sari of a self. Yet each strand, as it is foregrounded, gives the listener a 'different' story, a glimpse of a differently perceived and articulated self. I realize then, an important truth: as with the teaching and learning of music, as with the handing down from voice to ear to voice, the story of this life is woven at the moment of telling, for me, the listener, who will in her own way hear, tell and live out this story.

Is that the true meaning of the guru–shishya relationship? Does learning 'seena-ba-seena', 'heart-to-heart', mean that I, as shishya, listen with all my being to sounded and unsounded cadences of both music and life-story, then sing and tell and live out this music, this story, in my own way, in my own time, using the vocabulary of this rich strand and the many other hidden ones that go to make up my own never-quite-finished self?

≈≫ ≪≈

I realize then, that in the telling of the story I am more important than I had thought. I hear, I tell, a tale already twice told.

Many years ago, a girl was born. Her mother turned her face away. Years later, the baby is now the mother of a girl child. No one said mubarak to her at this birth. The first event, told to her, and the second come together now, in a single narrative, framed perhaps by my listening presence. Nainaji says, 'My mother was sad. She turned her face away. You see, I was the third girl.'

She tells me, 'I remember, I was holding the baby in my arms. All the servants looked down with morose faces. There was no rejoicing. There was no mubarak when my daughter June was born.'

She cradles an imaginary baby as she speaks. Suddenly the years are telescoped and I feel the warm weight of my own baby in my arms. My eyes are heavy with the fragmented sleep of a new mother. I feel again the special awed happiness at the birth of this tiny girl.

Is it to that newborn baby, June, that now, by hearing and living this story again, we accord, she and I, that delayed welcome? Or is it my daughter who through this story is alerted, ever so gently, to the realities of the world in which she must live? Is it the woman herself and her story that I hold in my arms, or is it a part of my own self, born just this minute?

Another day she says, 'In my parents' house women were treated with respect.' Her mother's sadness of which she spoke earlier—had I imagined it? Or does respect mean different things to different people? She is telling me now about the Brahmo Samaj, her father and her grandfather. The sadness of the mother of a third girl child has no place in this story.

Which story is true? Or are they both true? What is the relationship between the event as it happened and the event as it was told? The story as it was heard by me and then as told and written here? Which came first—the event or the story? Did she, like the Australian aborigines, bring into being her world, the events of her life by singing their names? Was the event given meaning, contextualized, by being stitched together with other seemingly disparate events, into a chosen narrative?

In a beautiful novella, *The Castle of Crossed Destinies*, Italo Calvino has his characters trace different stories from a single spread of the Tarot. Read upwards, downwards, diagonally, the cards reveal a new pattern, a new drama each time. By themselves, the cards, the events of a life, have little meaning. Juxtaposed in a chosen, consciously articulated pattern, they acquire meaning, order, a context. The pattern creates meaningful narratives. If so, denied the possibility of pattern-making, is a life doomed to be meaningless? When life, with all its suffering, is seen as a story, is it redeemed from absurdity and meaninglessness?

These are questions that can be answered in a hundred different ways, to make a hundred different story-patterns, and the possibilities would not be exhausted. For me, it is sufficient to say, today, for now, that the story of a life, like the making of a self, is perhaps, a constant process. A life is lived; it is its own brave story. Once 'told', even if only to oneself, it becomes meaningful. And it is never told in a vacuum. The moment of telling and receiving the story is equally its framer and narrator. The listener who will retell this twice-told tale fashions into it details of her own self and story, which are, themselves, involved in the unending process of making, unmaking, remaking themselves.

As I follow Nainaji from one space to the other, as song and story repeatedly weave together, I realize that for me they are not so different after all. And I understand why our interactions with each other are textured so richly.

Nor are we so different from all the other gurus and shishyas before and after us. In each case, story and song will both be handed down with trust, will be received with respect, will be retold and re-sung with an inner conviction. How else could I learn to live my life as listener, student, performer; how else learn to hold fast to my commitments as an artiste; how else hope to experience the great secret of anhad, the unheard sound, except through such an interaction?

In the beginning I am plagued by self doubt. She brushes aside my worries, and begins on a beautiful old dadra:

> *More naina laage unse, jiya chahe so kare.*
> *Samjhaat, samjhe ye nahi, lakh jatan kare*
> *Ab kaise kari aali, man dheer na dhare.*
>
> Having looked into the eyes of my love, what's left
> to do?
> A million ways I explain, to no avail, the folly of
> this love.
> But oh my friend, this restless heart!

There are commitments one must make to oneself and to one's truest love—what's left to say or do? Did she mean for me to hear and understand the bandish this way? When she tells me, as she often does, about her own life, is it to make sure that I understand?

'I was married when I was seventeen. In those days, women of "good families" did not sing. It was different in my father's house, but things changed for me when I got married. As a bahu of the Kapurthala rajwada, singing was out of the question. It was only after my husband died that a friend encouraged me to start singing again. I had to go through that tragedy to rediscover myself as an artiste.

'I might have become like many other women—comfortable, sociable, busy bringing up children and grandchildren—but life had other plans for me. Faced with tragedy, I too could have retreated into myself or become bitter, blaming life for the tricks it had played on me. Instead, in a strange way this became the turning point in my life. It seems to me that life gives us these crises, these challenges, so that we move on and find our true selves.'

The only music she heard in those days was at the mujras organized on special occasions—weddings, births and other celebrations. Professional women singers, tawaifs, would be invited to perform. 'Mujra means salaam,' says Nainaji, and to prove her point she pulls out a sheaf of crumbling yellowed paper. On the pages are printed in large Devanagari type, a series of song texts, bandishes. The page facing each bandish has the musical notation for it. Each song is identified according to genre—sohar, mehndi, banna-banni, ubatan, and each collection begins with an invocation, a mujra. Collected and printed by the late Nawab of Rampur, Raza Ali Khan—some of them his own compositions—Nainaji has preserved these carefully, one of the few witnesses to the abundance of forms sung at life cycle ceremonies and other rituals. 'Mujra is the singer's salaami, her respectful greeting to her patrons. Even now in many royal families a respectful greeting is accompanied by the word "mujra".'

But she is wandering from the main thread of her story and I bring her back to it as she so often brings me safely back to the mukhra of the bandish and to its sam, after setting me off on a foray into the unexpected rastas or improvisatory paths opening up in the thumri she is teaching me.

Mujras were the only occasions for her to listen to music.

'I longed to sing. We women were not permitted to attend mehfils; singing was out of the question. The women of the household invariably hated these mujras. Perhaps, they reminded them of their tenuous hold on their husbands' affections and attention. But unlike the other women, I was always happy when there was a mujra in the house. Sitting behind a screen, I could see and hear everything without myself being seen. And what wonderful singing and dancing I have witnessed!'

She tells me that several of the dadras and shers (Urdu verses) in her repertoire are the gift of these tawaifs. She would write down the bandishes, send for the singer after the mehfil, ask her to sing them again, and then store these treasures somewhere in her heart. But for what? She tells me, 'It was to be so long before I sang those verses. At the time I couldn't have imagined I would ever sing them, that I would become a singer.' Her eyes cloud over. 'My deepest wish to be a singer came true—but what strange twists of fate I had to endure!' Her fingers run lightly over the keys of her beautiful harmonium—one that has been used by Begum Akhtar, Bade Ghulam Ali Khan, Rasoolan Bai, Mushtaq Hussain Khan. She sings a sher, a memory preserved from a now almost forgotten singer, and begins to tell me about her.

As she speaks, I see Nainaji in my mind's eye—a young woman, a girl really, a teenager still. But this girl is married and is the mother of a baby girl. From behind her ornate chilman screen, she is watching the festivities to welcome the newborn. It is in Lucknow, in a house that had been bought before 1856, before Wajid Ali Shah was exiled from his naihar, and Awadh was annexed by the British. She stresses this repeatedly. The family was not one of those that rose to prominence after the old aristocracy had been exiled; the family was a very old, aristocratic one and loyal to the Nawab.

⇒⟫ ⟪⟸

Benazir Bai has been invited to perform. One of the most famous tawaifs of the time, she is truly benazir—peerless—utterly beautiful. Having suffered the scorn of artistes like Gauhar Jan, Benazir had resolved to take taleem from none other than Ustad Kale Khan of the Kirana gharana. Thus in addition to her charm and beauty she became a superlative artiste. Many years later, I will hear of Benazir Bai again, and this time from Shanti Hiranandji. She will tell me how Benazir khala—Aunt Benazir—now married and 'retired', would come to visit Begum Akhtar. The Begum would entreat and cajole her into singing the dadra for which she was justly famous—'*Niure niure buharai anganwa…*'

But in Nainaji's story, Benazir is still young, still centre stage, at the height of her career. From behind a screen, a young girl watches and listens enthralled as Benazir sings a dadra. In the style of those days, Benazir is moving about the mehfil, expressing the dadra also with her eyes and with hand movements in the bhav batana style. Her accompanists, instruments tied to their waists, follow her about. It is a typical Lucknow dadra, interspersed with shers and dohas: '*Haale dole mor jiyara*'—this tumultuous heart!

Now Benazir stops. The tabliya takes up the laggi, and the sarangiya plays the mukhra to this faster-paced sequence that comes at the end of the dadra. Benazir Bai begins to dance, not just bhav, not just with eyes and hands, but the scintillating, swift footwork—the laris and chakkars of Kathak. Watching from behind the screen, the girl holds her breath. The men in the audience exclaim 'Wah! Wah!' and shower Benazir with coins and jewellery.

Standing in that shower of gold, Benazir begins another song—a ghazal—at the request of one of her listening admirers. 'It was a favourite of his,' Nainaji tells me. 'Every time Benazir Bai was invited to sing, he would ask for this ghazal.'

At his request Benazir begins. As Nainaji sings it, I realize that its rather trite lyrics mask a deep pain, mask thoughts and feelings that Benazir and women like her might never have expressed except thus indirectly:

> *Kahin bhi, kisi se mohabbat na karna.*
>
> Don't ever fall in love, never, not with anyone.

Whom was Benazir warning, I wonder. Herself? Women like her who knew, so achingly, so sharply, that this mohabbat is only something to sing about, never to experience?

Then there is a pause, while the men go in to dine. In that pause, Benazir Bai gives in to fatigue. She stands limp and exhausted in the room. She looks at her sarangiya. He puts aside his instrument and coming up to her and massages her back and legs. From behind the screen the girl watches. She will never forget this sight—Benazir's ethereal beauty collapsing into something close to coarseness, and yet her vulnerability, the bond between her and her sarangiya. She watches, deeply hurt, almost disgusted at the sight of this fairylike creature being touched, and so intimately, by this old, rather ugly man. The realities of her own marriage and

motherhood have not yet robbed her of her romantic notions
of fairy queens and prince charmings. Yet she cannot tear
her eyes away.

Many years later, Nainaji will meet Benazir again. Benazir
is a married woman now. She does not sing any more. 'Don't
you miss singing?' Nainaji will ask her. 'Don't you ever feel
you'd like to perform again?' And Benazir will smile gently
and speak of the need to survive: 'Once that was my source
of sustenance; now my marriage looks after me.'

I think I understand why she is telling me this story. I
realize I have just learnt something important about the
singing of thumri.

I recall a recent lesson. She has taught me a dadra in raga
Pilu:

> *Aiso jatan bataye daiyo Ram*
> *Kaise din kati hain.*

> Tell me how shall I pass these days?

This mood of biraha, the pain of separation from the
loved one, cradled in the sweet notes of Pilu is interrupted
by a rather grisly doha:

> *Kaaga sab tan khaiyo, aur chun chun khaiyo maas*
> *In do nainan mat khaiyo kaaga, mohe piya milan ki aas*

> Peck at this flesh, devour this body, crow.
> Only spare these eyes
> That long for a vision of the Beloved.

The sensuousness of this dadra, the savouring of the rasa
of viyog shringar, of love in separation, does not exclude a
knowledge and acceptance of this horrible image. If shringar
can be expressed through sorrow, karuna, then bhayanaka

and vibhatsa, the terrifying and the gruesome are not alien to its expression. How often has Nainaji told me, 'Thumri is about love.' I realize that love has been romanticized so much that we have almost forgotten its texture. But thumri, seemingly the most romantic of all musical forms, presents the careful listener with love's other faces—the angers and cruelties, the grotesqueness, the absurdity as well as the tenderness and caring, the poetry and laughter. 'Shringar is so vast,' Nainaji has told me, 'ranging from the sensuous to the sublime. That is why the colour of shringar is blue—the blue of the sky and the ocean, the blue of Infinity.'

It was different in her father's house where music was a part of everyday life. 'All of us children sang, or played some instrument. And not just us—there was a photograph of my aunts taken in 1889 each playing an instrument, making music together. My aunts knew all the popular bandishes and thumris.' She tells me how an aunt used to sing, and had taught her the classic Khamaj thumri—'*Kaun gali gayo Shyam*'. And when I ask her about the bandishes of Nawab Wajid Ali Shah, she tells me, as she teaches me, how her mother used to sing the Nawab's lament:

> *Jab chhod chale Lucknow nagari*
> *Tab haal Ali par kya guzri*
> *Mahal mahal mein begum roye,*
> *Jab hum guzre, duniya guzri.*

> Imagine Ali's suffering
> When Lucknow was abandoned!
> In the palaces the begums weep
> A world comes to an end with my passing.

Then she would break off and explain to me that thumri, travelled to Calcutta (now Kolkata) with the exiled Nawab of Awadh. Wajid Ali Shah, the deposed Nawab was exiled by the British in 1858. Mourning this moment, this ruler, who was a fine poet, composer, singer and dancer, had spontaneously burst into a beautiful thumri. This song, apparently in the voice of the young bride leaving her parental home forever, is the Nawab's own swan song, his lament at having to leave forever the land of his ancestors and travel, an exile now, to an unknown city.

> *Babul mora naihar chhooto hi jaye*
> *Char kahar mile, mori doliya sajaayi*
> *Mora apna begaana chooto jaye.*
> *Angana to parbat bhaya aur deori bhayi bides*
> *Le babul ghar aapna, main chali piya ke des.*

> My father, your home slips away from me.
> You found four palanquin-bearers, decorated my doli
> Now all that was once familiar, loved, slips away.
> Your courtyard, now an insurmountable mountain;
> Its threshold a foreign land.
> Father, to you your house;
> I set out for my husband's land.

Interestingly, there is some controversy as so whether Wajid Ali Shah did indeed compose '*Babul mora*': one giveaway clue is the extremely slow tempo and elongated avartan (time cycle) of this bandish that is more typical of the style that developed around the 1930s. On the other hand, '*Jab chhod chale*' seems to have been a staple of Brahmo households—even finding its way into Satyajit Ray's film *Shatranj ke Khiladi* which has at its heart the exile of the Nawab of Awadh to Matiaburj.

The exiled Wajid Ali Shah set up court at Matiaburj, near Calcutta. With him had come a retinue of courtiers, but also, singers, dancers, poets, actors, cooks and craftsmen. The styles and forms performed at the Matiaburj court-in-exile, spilled over to neighbouring Calcutta, and became an intrinsic part of that city's artistic landscape.

The Sens encouraged their children, two boys and three girls to sing, dance, act and write. It was all part of the new notion of education, both for the individual and for the nascent nation. Education, including a knowledge of the arts, would help their children, daughters too, to become more able human beings, better equipped to fulfil their given role in life. The Sens would, however, never have dreamt of a future for their daughters that included professional performance. A woman's role was believed to be that of the good wife and mother, one who would not only be an able and intelligent companion to her husband and a loving guide to her children, future citizens, but one who would be able to extend these qualities out into the world without compromising her 'womanly' nature. A liberal education would help her achieve this and thereby help society and the nation. It was a vision that Nilina's parents had inherited from Keshub Chandra Sen, and one that inspired many in early twentieth century Bengal.

And so, Nilina went to school, uncommon for girls in those days, first to the Loretto Convent and then to the Victoria Institute in Calcutta. And she grew up listening to, and participating in music.

'Our house was always full of music. My elder brother, Sunith, loved music and would regularly organize concerts

of the great artistes of those days—Enayat Khan, Mehdi
Hussain Khan, Girija Shankar Chakravarty—but because
of my grandfather's deeply religious bent of mind and his
approach to life, no mehfils of professional women singers
were ever organized in our house. Furthermore, the women
of the family were not allowed to attend the mehfils. Yet,
despite this rule, my brother would let me sit with him and
listen—after all I was so very young. So I grew up listening
to very good music. I owe that to my brother.'

In her grandfather's disapproval of professional women
singers, I hear an echo of the controversy surrounding
the introduction of these performers into the new theatre
of Bengal. Ishwar Chandra Vidyasagar had withdrawn his
support to theatre in protest against this move. Amateur
theatricals where women participated was a different matter,
as was the public stage where men played women's roles. The
Sens shared this attitude.

Despite this, Nainaji heard the professional women singers
too.

She laughs as she recalls the first time she witnessed
a naach of the tawaifs. I see her, as she speaks, a little
eight-year-old peering down from a jharokha in a house
called Emerald Bower in Calcutta. This house too has been
part of Calcutta's changing story. A stately home of the Tagore
family—it was built by Harakumar Tagore—it later became
the campus of the Indian Institute of Management. Today
it is back, in a sense, with the Tagores; it is now owned by
Visva Bharati University, Santiniketan.

But back to Nainaji's story. The child is watching a
naach. She has insisted on being taken to this rather grand
reception for the Nawab and Begum of Rampur at which
the viceroy and the vicereine were also to be present. The

reception is being hosted by the zamindar, musicologist and music patron, Raja Prodyut Kumar Tagore, grandson of Harakumar Tagore, and members of Calcutta's elite, the Sens included, have been invited.

'I saw the card when it came to the house. It said that my parents were invited to a banquet, and that following the banquet there was to be a naach. And I begged to be allowed to go with them. My parents refused flatly. "This is not a party for children," they said. But I cried and pleaded. I even came up with a solution to the problem of how to smuggle a small child into a formal banquet-cum-reception in the glittering days of the Raj. The Nawab and the Begum of Rampur had come to Calcutta for the occasion and were staying at Emerald Bower as the Raja Saheb's guests. My mother had taken me with her one day when she had gone to meet the Begum Saheba. I told my mother, "I can stay with Begum Saheba while you go for dinner and I can watch the naach with her." I pleaded so hard that finally my parents gave in. And that is how I saw the naach at Emerald Bower.'

The Begum was in strict parda. Nainaji was taken by her mother to the Begum's apartments. She tells me, 'I still remember that the doors were guarded by two eunuchs holding spears.' The Begum Saheba welcomed the pretty little girl, they had dinner together, and the child, tired after her tantrums and all the excitement, curled up and went to sleep.

In another part of the house, the elite of Calcutta had gathered for the banquet. Then, after dinner:

'Suddenly, in my sleep, I heard the plaintive sound of sarangis and the jingle of ghunghroos. I sat bolt upright, sleep vanished in a second, wide awake—this was what I had come for! I rushed to the jharokha. The rooms on the

first floor looked onto the well of a ballroom. I saw the
tawaifs coming in one by one, making salaam to the mehfil
and curtsying to the viceroy and the vicereine. They were
all there, the famous tawaifs of those days. Begum Saheba
pointed them out to me. Rattan Bai, much-feted star of the
play *Yehudi ki Ladki*; she was wearing a magenta peshwaz
studded with salma work, and her hair fell well below her
knees. Jaddan Bai, mother of the film star Nargis, and a
famous singer of her time was there too. So was Janki Bai
Chhappan Chhuri, whose beautiful face had been slashed
with fifty-six knife strokes by a jealous lover, hence her
name. Gauhar Jan, arrogant, witty, queen of the tawaifs of
her time was there, so was Angurbala, Chulbule Wali Malka.
These women sang and danced in ways that will never be
heard or seen again. It was their way of life—bol banana,
bhav batana, addressing each person in the audience directly.
I heard thumris, dadras, tappas, ghazals, saw aamad, thaat,
tatkar, bhav, chakkars, parans... And then—they began
to sing English songs—"*K-K-K-Katy, My Beautiful Katy*"
and "*Oh, Johnny, Johnny*"! They had to sing something to
please everyone.'

As she speaks, I remember something I had read in an old
newspaper of the 1930s, about a music festival in Allahabad.
The writer had mentioned Janki Bai Chhapan Chhuri, waiting
in the wings for her turn to go on stage. She sat there, a large
woman with a scarred face, chewing paan, waiting. But what
had struck the writer were the medals pinned to her saree,
and the pride with which she displayed them. When it was
her turn to sing, Janki Bai ended her concert of thumris and
dadras with an English song: '*My love is like a little bird, that
flits from tree to tree ...*' To the writer of that piece, Janki
Bai, her medals, 'the strange wailing sounds' of the 'native

songs', especially her attempt to sing an English song were something to be mocked and ridiculed. But the Janki Bai I know, the one Nainaji tells me about, is memorable for her indomitable will, a woman who wore the scars of a terrible encounter as a badge of courage, one among the many medals that adorned her shoulder. She is memorable too as a fine composer of bandishes, as a reciter (who also recorded) of the unusual forms of naat, soz and marsiya. As Nainaji speaks, I remember all this, and I hear Janki Bai's voice bright and clear through the hissing background of a 78 rpm recording: '*Shyam ki re bajana laage baansuri*' (Shyam's flute, my friend, begins to sound).

Later, there would be other times, when Nainaji heard the music of the tawaifs:

'In those days, as today, Banaras was an important centre of music and especially of thumri. My grandmother lived in Banaras. She had gone there to live out her last days and to die in the sacred city. Many Bengali widows used to do that. I was often taken to her home during my summer holidays. Who could be in Banaras for even a single day and not hear thumri? I was there in early summer when there were festivities and singing at the Shitala temple and on the river for Burhwa Mangal. This was also the time of the Gulab Bari festival.'

The Shitala temple stands small and red, close to the Dasaswamedh Ghat. On one of my own trips to Banaras, a boatman tells me that there is no singing here any more, not by tawaifs anyway.

Nainaji tells me, 'The tawaifs always sang for Shitala Mata, asking for her blessings, asking the terrible goddess of smallpox for the gifts of health and beauty, seeking to cool her anger with their music.'

My boatman had said: 'After Shitalashtami comes the summer heat and then the rains. The river rises so high that the Shitala temple is submerged; Shitala Mata's anger is cooled.'

On the first Tuesday of the month of Chaitra, Banaras would celebrate the Burhwa Mangal festival. Rajas, Nawabs and rich patrons would sit on decorated boats on the Ganga, their favourite singers with them. The river would be transformed into a floating stage, the singers' voices touching the highest notes—the teep ke swar—their songs mingling, one with the other, flowing into each other.

At both this festival and the Gulab Bari festival, the favoured forms were chaiti and ghato. These folk-derived seasonal forms, sung during the lazy days of early summer, are based on dhuns related to the ragas Jogiya, Pahari, Tilak Kamod and Pilu. Of all the styles in the thumri repertoire, chaiti is perhaps the most sensuous. As she teaches me a chaiti, Nainaji tells me, 'Chaiti comes after the boisterous playfulness of the horis and rasiyas of the preceding season of Basant, or spring. It evokes the voice and emotions of the rati-tripta nayika, heavy-eyed and langorous after love's consummation.' The nayika sings then:

Chait ki nindiya, jiyara alsaane, ho Ram!

How drowsy, how lazy, I feel in Chait!

⇢⟫ ⟪⇠

How did she begin her taleem? I ask her one day and she tells me this story: Her brother had organized a mehfil in their house. The singer was Girija Shankar Chakravarty, the legendary artiste. The son of a famous lawyer of Murshidabad, Girija Babu was the disciple of great masters such as Radhika

Prasad Goswami, Bhaiya Ganpat Rao and Moujuddin Khan, Muzaffar Khan and Mohammad Ali Khan, Wazir Khan, Inayat Hussain Khan and Badal Khan. Nainaji tells me, 'His gayaki was a unique and aesthetic blend of the finest qualities of the Murshidabad, Gwalior, Banaras, Tanras Khan (Dilli), Rampur and Agra gharanas. The depth of his understanding of music and his command over Hindi and Urdu can be seen in the many beautiful khayal and thumri bandishes he composed.' She reminds me now of one of these—the beautiful Jogiya thumri, *'Saiyan na laaye gavanawa'*.

That long ago night, Nainaji knew nothing of this. But young though she was she sensed that she was in the presence of an extraordinary artiste. She sat listening, spellbound.

Girija Babu sang all night and as dawn broke, he ended his recital with a wistful Bhairavi thumri:

> *Bansiya bajaaye, mor jiya ko lubhaaye*
> *Has has garwa lagaaye.*
> *Sapnon mein Shyam sang kati rain saari*
> *Ab bairan bhor jagaaye.*

> Playing his flute, entrancing me,
> Laughing, he holds me close.
> Thus, dreaming, the night was spent with Shyam.
> Now dawn, my enemy, awakens me.

The last notes, then silence. In the silence, like an after-image, Bhairavi echoes in the room. Outside, night's darkness yields to the first soft pink of a perfidious dawn; music's dream time is over. The mehfil begins to stir and stretch, reluctant to let go of the state of sama, the spell the singer has cast.

Girija Babu picks up the little five-year-old who has sat listening so seriously through a whole night of music. 'So what did you like best?' he asks her playfully. 'Your Bhairavi,' she answers, very serious. 'Oh!' he says, controlling his laughter. 'And can you sing Bhairavi for me?' She sings then, in a sweet, clear voice, echoing the thumri he has just sung.

Girija Babu hugs the little girl and makes her his shagird that very day. She will learn from him for nine years and his ang will be with her for life. So faithful will her singing be to his style that years later, a sarangiya in Lucknow, Laddan Khan, wondering at this andaz will ask her if she is Suraj's child, Suraj being the daughter of Girija Babu and his beloved Chandravali.

3

Naba Brindaban

When Nainaji was born, much had already happened to transform Calcutta from a group of three small villages into the bustling city it became in the nineteenth century. Though the capital had shifted to Delhi, the Calcutta of Nainaji's childhood remained an important centre of British interests, and also the hub of Indian and British intellectual and artistic activity, social reform and nationalist thought.

The debates generated in the eighteenth and nineteenth centuries by the Orientalists on the one hand and the Utilitarians and Evangelists on the other, and by Indian writings of similar and other persuasion had crystallized into clear maps of the past and ideologies for the future. An important area to be addressed was the status of women. By the early years of the twentieth century many issues like women's education, widow remarriage and raising of the age of marriage had already been legislated upon, though debate continued. The Bengal that was Nainaji's home, had been divided in 1905. That division had been opposed and then rescinded. The early proto-nationalist ideas of the nineteenth century had paved the way for a full-fledged, though not homogenous, nationalist movement. At another level, impoverished artisans and folk artistes from Calcutta's hinterland had poured into the developing city in search of a livelihood, bringing with them their own bold, vibrant art forms and song styles. In nearby, Matiaburj, the exiled Nawab of Lucknow, Wajid Ali Shah, had set up court, creating, in that far-off land, a miniature Awadh. With him came a retinue of singers, dancers, bhands and poets whose performances were to greatly influence the cultural life of Calcutta. Thus, the tappa style of singing, brought to Purab from Multan by Mian Shori, found followers among local artistes. One of them was Ramnidhi Gupta or Nidhu Babu as he was popularly known. Nidhu Babu adapted the tappa style to create the Bengali tappa. This style also fostered a style of Bangla devotional music called Shyama Sangeet, songs sung in praise of Kali. Thumri itself, the style par excellence of Wajid Ali Shah's court, became a popular style with singers in Calcutta. These singers—tawaifs or baijis—were in great demand to perform at puja celebrations, life-cycle festivities and also at formal banquets and receptions.

All these influences were to become strands in the story of Nainaji's life. One strand in particular was very significant: the influence of the Brahmo Samaj and of her paternal grandfather, Keshub Chandra Sen.

Keshub Chandra Sen was born into a 'respectable' Vaishnava family of the Vaidya caste in 1838, ten years after Raja Rammohun Roy first founded the Brahmo Samaj. Sen had begun his association with the Brahmo Samaj as a dynamic and radical young follower and close associate of Debendranath Tagore. Like that of his compatriots, his vision encompassed a revitalizing of Indian society and culture by a simultaneous recovery of its 'pure' past and a surge forward into an 'enlightened' future. Yet, he differed increasingly with Debendranath Tagore in his vision of the Samaj as not just a religious organization, but as one that would also spearhead social reform.

By the 1860s and 70s Sen had risen to prominence in the Samaj and was formulating a discourse on women that was to influence the course of history. This discourse was also, as it now appears to us, riven with contradictions. The Brahmo Samaj argued forcefully for reform for women—opposing sati and child marriage, pleading for women's education and widow remarriage. Yet it gave women a clearly separate space, ideologically and even physically. Thus, while Sen was in favour of education for women, he was clear that its content and purpose had to be different from the education given to men. Nor did Sen approve of women mixing freely with men, or even sitting outside the purdah area during the Brahmo prayer service. He believed that a woman's primary role was that of wife and mother. It was therefore quite unnecessary, he wrote, even harmful, for women to study mathematics, science and philosophy. He believed that they should, ideally, study the ancient texts which would instruct them in the role and duties of a good wife. He urged them to uphold the 'brata ideals' of women like Savitri. For those women aspiring to education and knowledge, there were the brata ideals of Maitreyi and Lilavati.

Not everyone in the Samaj agreed with Sen. Eventually conflicts within the Samaj came to a head over the controversy associated with the marriage of Sen's daughter, Suniti Debi, to the Maharaja of Cooch Behar.

The dust raised by that storm has not quite settled in Nainaji's mind. She often refers to this controversy, attempting to explain it. It has an immediacy for her, as if it happened yesterday.

Many in the Brahmo Samaj had criticized this marriage,

seeing it as a reneging of Brahmo tenets on social and religious reform. Sen had drafted the Indian Marriage Act a year earlier. This Act prohibited the marriage of women under fourteen years of age, and sought to introduce a new Brahmo form of marriage that did away with rituals. The Cooch Behar marriage, it was said, made a mockery of the new Act, as Suniti Debi was under fourteen. Sen's detractors also argued that to please the bridegroom's relatives, certain Hindu rituals and ritual objects had been incorporated into the marriage ceremony. Sen defended his actions saying the ceremony had been a betrothal only, not a wedding. An associate argued that no ritual performed could be construed as anti-Brahmo. These are arguments I still hear from Nainaji, who believes that the controversy over the marriage was deliberately created 'by my grandfather's enemies who were jealous of him'. Various accusations were levelled at Sen by his detractors: that he had gone against his own beliefs and arranged this marriage because his son-in-law was from a royal family, that he had succumbed to pressure and allowed a Hindu ceremony, that the bride was under age.

Sen and his friends defended their position. Sen repeatedly writes about himself as being utterly other-worldly, not in the least interested in money or social position. Nainaji echoes this. His insistence on marrying his daughter into the Cooch Behar family, she tells me, was altruistic—to ensure that through her, education and social reform would spread to this area as well: 'My aunt worked tirelessly for women's education. She also tried to stop the large-scale migration of musicians from Cooch Behar to other parts of India by providing patronage right there.' She names several musicians. 'Originally their ancestors were from Cooch Behar,' she says. Nainaji defends the ceremony: 'It was a betrothal only.

After the ceremony my aunt came back to Calcutta, and the Maharaja went to England for his education. It was only two years later, when my aunt was sixteen, that the marriage was performed.'

Betrothal or marriage, one thing is certain, that the Cooch Behar affair reflected a pattern that was not an isolated one in the Sen family. Marriages between Brahmo Samajis and Sanatani Hindus was an issue that could not easily be avoided as might be gleaned from the fact that contemporary novels often have such a crisis as one of their key elements. And despite Sen's protestations over the Cooch Behar controversy, several women of the family, daughters and granddaughters like Nainaji—married the sons of royal houses. One aunt was married to the ruler of Mayurbhanj, a sister married the raja of the Chakmas, and Nainaji herself was married into the royal family of Kapurthala.

I have asked her about her own marriage many, many times. How had she married into a family so different from her own? How could she have borne without sorrow, anger, despair, or a sense of injustice, the long years of silence imposed on her by her role as a wife?

Each time Nainaji speaks, I hear a slightly different answer. I hear these answers with my own changing awareness; each time I listen, I hear something just a little different. A flicker of a murki here, a note held a fraction of a second longer than I had thought. Was that how she said it the last time, or do I hear it differently now, or is it perhaps a bit of both?

One day she had said, 'I was becoming too interested in music. My mother did not want that to happen.'

I ask her why that should have been a concern. Sometimes

she doesn't reply. Sometimes she shrugs and says, 'Music wasn't something a woman of a "respectable" family could have pursued as a career. My parents would never have permitted me to perform in public.'

In her parents' home, however, she could listen to music, and she could learn from the great Girija Babu. All that stopped abruptly when she married.

'How did you feel? Not to be able to sing?' I ask, baffled, trying to tease out a hint of some anger or sorrow somewhere.

'I missed my music,' she says. 'But I was busy with my children, my new life, playing my role of hostess at the many parties arranged by my husband and my father-in-law.'

Then I remember another woman, another story.

A woman, who had been a singer at the court of Baroda once told me: 'A nobleman visiting Baroda, heard me sing and fell in love with me. But when I married him I could not sing any more. It was unheard of that the wife of a nobleman should be seen or heard singing. But then there were the children to look after, the household to run.... I was so busy. The years flew past. Where was the time to miss music?'

Then as she speaks further, now about her family, her daughter, she tells me about the time when, now an elderly grandmother in a very changed world, she had walked into her daughter's house to hear her granddaughter practising raga Todi on the sitar: 'I began to sing—after so many years. I had forgotten nothing. I sang and sang all morning, and then I fainted, overcome with emotion and exhaustion.'

There is a hint of tears in her eyes. My throat is choked as I ask again about those silent years. But the story is over. She looks at me, smiling—did I imagine the tears?—'I was so busy then, there was so much to do, the children, the household....'

-»>> «<-

Nainaji's father, Saral Chandra Sen, was the ninth of Keshub
Chandra Sen's ten children. He was eight years old when
Keshub Chandra Sen died, but even so, Nainaji believes,
his father's influence on him was great. Saral Babu was the
only one of Sen's children who continued to live at Lily
Cottage, Keshub Chandra Sen's house in Calcutta, which
later became the Victoria Institute for Girls. He trained
as a barrister but refused to practice law because, Nainaji
tells me, 'he believed that it required a man to tell lies and
so he settled instead for a job in the administrative set-
up.' At home, Saral Babu continued his father's practise of
performing such rituals as the Naba Sankirtans to celebrate
Maghotsav, the staging of plays like *Vidhava Vivah* and *Naba
Brindaban*. A process that had been started by Sen, and for
which he had been criticized—that of having 'Hinduized the
Samaj'—was perhaps becoming more crystallized in Saral
Babu's continuation of this tradition.

Nainaji shows me photographs of Lily Cottage and
the 'devalaya' built by her grandfather and tells me: 'At
Maghotsav, we would have Naba Sankirtan. Also, at this
festival, ten days would be dedicated to various people and
groups. On the first day we would have matribhoomi seva,
then ghar seva. These would be followed by days dedicated
to the service of parents, servants and even enemies. It was
to teach us the values of service, patriotism and forgiveness.
Also it was during Maghotsav that my father and brothers
and many others would participate in the sankirtans by
singing and dancing in processions. As they came home we
would be able to hear the cries of 'Hari Bol' and the clapping
of hands. They would return elated and tired to Lily Cottage;

my sisters and I would be waiting for them and would shower
them with rose petals as they entered the house. That day we
would serve them a special meal—fish, aloo dum and other
delicacies served on pale green banana leaves. We would
serve the men first and then we would eat. "Feed the brutes
first!" my mother would say with characteristic humour.'

⇒》 《⇐

Around the late 1870s, Keshab Chandra Sen had shifted from
the Samaj's more 'rational' position on religion to focus on a
new type of Brahmoism that incorporated ecstatic religious
experience, bhakti, and a belief in a universal religious
ideology which would be a synthesis of all religions. Festivals
like Maghotsav can be traced back to the 1880s when Sen
had begun to focus on this new type of Brahmoism. Sen led
processions through the streets of Calcutta bearing flags and
musical instruments, and singing hymns in the imagined
fashion of Chaitanya's devotional Vaishnavism. It was at this
time that Sen also began to experiment with what he called
'pilgrimages to the prophets'—sadhu samagams—which were
a continuation of his search for a universal, syncretic religious
form. In the sadhu samagams, a prophet or a teacher would
be chosen—Chaitanya Mahaprabhu or Moses, or someone
else. Tableaux would be set up depicting his life, and songs
and plays would be performed to illustrate his philosophy.
Thus, the participating audience would be drawn into a
highly charged, almost evangelical experience of a religion
or philosophy.

About her grandfather, Nainaji says: 'He was a rare person,
a great thinker, one who thought far ahead of his times. All
that he said is as relevant today as it was then.' She is referring
particularly to that aspect of Sen's thinking that she herself

has deeply internalized—his search for and passionate belief in a universal syncretic religion. She shows me what Sen had written: 'Let all sects retain their distinctive peculiarities, and yet let them unite in fraternal alliance.' This finds expression in her own beliefs and in her writing: '...each voice retains its peculiar tone, yet out of the union of many voices and diverse instruments comes forth sweet music.'

Her dedication to this idea finds expression in the many programmes she had organized. Most significant of these, perhaps, was the seminar-cum-festival Bansuri, organized in 1980 in collaboration with the Sangeet Natak Akademi and the Sahitya Kala Parishad. Bansuri explored through performances of music and dance, and through talks and discussions, the influence of Sufism and Vaishnavism on Indian music. Naina Devi defined the conceptual framework of Bansuri thus:

'Music is not merely a means of entertainment but probably the best instrument of communion with the Ultimate. It is interesting to note that bansuri or the flute plays an important part in both Vaishnavite and Sufi thought. The call of the soul is symbolized by it…. Krishna was inseparable from his flute and the magic of his flute was irresistible to the gopis of Brajbhumi. This theme has given rise to many musical forms extant today. The flute has played an equally vital role in Sufism. Maulana Jalaluddin Rumi started his Mathnavi with the flute, called "nei" in Persian.'

Sufi philosophy, poetry and music are centre-stage today, but the dancer Shovana Narayan reminds me that 'Nainaji was the first person in the art world to highlight the significance of Sufi philosophy, the links between Sufism and Vaishnavism, and the influence of both philosophies on Indian art traditions.'

Yet another programme that Nainaji organized, Kartik
Mahima, is a recreation, through song and dance, of the
customs, myths and legends that surround Kartik Purnima.
A particularly auspicious day, Kartik Purnima, is the day of
the cattle fairs at Sonepur and Pushkar; it is the day when
devout Hindus bathe in sacred rivers and lakes. It is a harvest
festival when people thank the earth for her bounty. It is
the day when Vishnu rescued the Vedas from the demon
Shankhasura, and when he delivered Gajendra, the elephant
king, from the jaws of the crocodile. It commemorates Shiva's
victory over the demon Tripurasura. Gurpurab, the birthday
of Guru Nanak falls on the same day. Tulsi puja is performed
by women in the days before Kartik Purnima to celebrate
Tulsi's chastity and Vishnu's love for this woman. From
Sharad Purnima to Kartik Purnima is the time of Krishna's
sensuous raas in the never-never-land of Brindavan. And
Kartik Purnima is also the festival of both tawaifs and
prostitutes. Even today prostitutes in Calcutta make images
of Kartik that, interestingly, in an earlier time resembled the
nineteenth-century babus of the Kalighat paintings; now they
are modelled on cinema stars. Paddy, pulses and barley are
sown and left to germinate, linking Kartik and the prostitutes
with the regeneration and fertility of the earth and of human
beings. So while Kartik Purnima has strong associations
with Vaishnava traditions and legends, it is also associated
with older cults: fertility rites, female chastity, worship
of the earth and her fruit, worship of and trade in cattle,
worship of Shiva and Kartik…. Nainaji's Kartik Mahima
draws on many of these stories to make a series of loosely
connected narratives which are presented through song and
dance sequences. Through these she hopes to acquaint 'the
younger generation with our traditions,' to encourage them

'to understand the real meaning behind these stories and customs' and to emphasize that a syncretic culture and an integrated society 'is something we have always had in the past, and have only now lost. Integration is a heritage of the performing arts.'

Thus Kartik Mahima not only depicts the rescue by Vishnu of the Vedas, but also has sequences of Nazir Akbarabadi's nazms in praise of Guru Nanak and the pranks of the child Krishna. 'Nazir, an eighteenth century poet of Agra, a Muslim, could equally love and worship Krishna and Nanak. People were not narrow-minded and sectarian in those days,' she says.

In the sequence '*Tulsa rani aaye gayi more angana*', Nainaji shows women singing and worshipping Tulsi. The song itself is composed like a banni, a bridal song that describes the bride's beauty, her clothes and her jewellery, thus linking puranic myths with secular household music.

In the poem '*Khelat raas*' set in raga Pilu in the thumri ang, Krishna and two gopis dance to this song against a painted backdrop of arched windows, trellises and jharokhas. An angan wall frames the dancers, while a painted leafy tree brings the pastoral world of Brindavan into this courtly ambience creating a multilayered visual. The legend of Krishna's raas is relocated here in the world of an eighteenth century miniature, itself painted with the brush of nostalgia by Nainaji's vision of this world and this raas.

This raas and indeed all of Kartik Mahima is a representation that echoes Keshub Chandra Sen's sense of myths and rites as allegories of spiritual truths. There is a deeper meaning that Nainaji, like her grandfather before her, wishes to uncover, through the aesthetics of dance and music, those visible, tangible modes through which these truths can be expressed and understood. 'After all,' as she often says, quoting the Bhagavat Purana, 'it is music and dance that redeem us in Kali Yuga.'

Yet, Sen's own attitude to theatre and the performing arts was highly ambivalent. On the one hand, there was his stern hostility to all vices which included not only gambling, prostitution, opium smoking, social drinking and playing cards, but also going to the theatre. On the other hand, Sen used theatre, song and dance as an integral part of his sadhu samagams and other religio-intellectual exercises. His staging of *Vidhava Vivaha* in 1857 was the first use of drama as a vehicle for social reform. He had also produced *Naba Brindaban*, an allegorical play about the harmony of life and Indian culture. He had acted in the play himself, while the part of Vivek was played by a young boy called Narendra Nath Datta, whom the world would know later as Swami Vivekananda. Certainly Sen's method of incorporating these elements in a didactic fashion, using them as a panacea to solve social problems, justified, in his view, his use of them. Moreover, Sen's objection was to professional theatre and to professional performers, especially professional performing women, not to theatre per se.

Many of Sen's ideas lived on, in some form or other, in Lily Cottage. Saral Babu encouraged his children to sing, dance and act. Nainaji tells me how her father, in turn, staged *Naba Brindaban*. 'This time I was Vivek,' she says, and tells me how Vivekananda had written to Saral Babu expressing his happiness that Sen's good work was being continued.

The house was always full of music: 'My brothers would organize mehfils of the leading male singers—Girija Babu, Enayat Khan and others—but none of the tawaifs. We children had our own orchestra, Prodeep, my younger brother played the violin. I would sing, Mejdi [Sadhona] would dance, and Didi [Benita] would write plays for us to perform. Taking up dance or music as a profession however was out of the question. Even Mejdi, so as not to jeopardize my chances of finding a good match, did not become a professional actress until after I was married—and even then, my parents disapproved strongly of her decision. But we were always social rebels and Mejdi became a professional dancer and stage actress and later entered the world of films.'

For Nainaji herself, the jump from housewife to professional singer came later.

→》》 《《←

Nainaji's mother Nirmala, or Nellie as she was called, was one of nine children. Her family were shipping magnates from Chittagong, but her own father, like so many ambitious young men of the time, took his degree in law and became a barrister. He moved to Burma (now Myanmar) where he set up a flourishing practice, bought property in Rangoon, and became the Administrator General of Burma. Nellie's brothers, following in their father's footsteps, also took up law as profession.

'You would have loved her,' Nainaji says to me, speaking of her mother: 'She was an open, warm-hearted person. She had a terrible temper too, but her outbursts would last just five seconds. She had a great sense of humour and was always ready to try something new. Soon after she was married she went to England with my father where she not only learnt ice skating, but won a prize in a competition!'

She had great inner strength too. Nellie was the centre of the family. Rena Singh, Nainaji's daughter tells me one day, 'We all, my mother included, leaned on her, drew strength from her. Didima, my grandmother, was like the Rock of Gibraltar.'

But the story that has passed into family history is this. In 1905, soon after the partition of Bengal, the Prince of Wales, later George V, visited Calcutta. 'As one of Calcutta's important families, the Maharaja and Maharani of Cooch Behar invited him to tea. The Maharani of Cooch Behar, was of course, none other than Suniti Debi, Nainaji's pishi or father's sister, over whose marriage there had been so much controversy. Also invited were the newly-married couple, Saral Babu and his wife, the rest of the family and several other important people.

'My aunt dressed my mother in a beautiful magenta saree, from her wedding trousseau. That saree belongs now to my sister-in-law Alo, Prodeep's wife. Ma was very pretty—she must have looked beautiful then. After tea, the Prince of Wales asked her to sing. Ma had no inhibitions. She sat down at the piano—a standard item in many Brahmo households—and began to sing a Bengali love song with (for this occasion) a hidden political meaning: "If you don't care for me, why do you come here pretending to love me?" '

It was impossible, of course, for a family like the Sens to be isolated from the nationalist movement. On one occasion, teaching the singers Suhasini Koratkar and Vinay Bhide Nidhu Babu's version of 'Vande Mataram', Nainaji recalled how, in 1932, she had sung it at the inauguration of the Indian National Congress in Calcutta. This version is set in Des raga in tappa ang—Nidhu Babu's favourite style. 'This was the first tune, the original tune of this song,' she says. 'Nidhu Babu had set it to this tune and Bankimchandra had himself heard it and approved.'

Now remembering that, I wonder how Nainaji would have

responded to the recent controversy over the singing of this
song. What would she have thought, what would she have
said? She who was always so generous, so fair and so inclusive
of 'the other' in everything that she said and did—how would
she have responded to this terrible controversy over a song
that she loved so dearly? As I think about that, I recall my
own brush with the song at the height of the controversy.
Invited to conduct a music workshop at a school, I was
greeted when I arrived with the singing of '*Vande Mataram*'
by the children. The children were from the primary school,
and were not old enough to have understood any aspect of
the controversy that was raging over the compulsory singing
of the song in schools. Yet I had felt I could not let the issue
go by without some discussion; I did not wish to belittle or
reject the children's musical offering either. Taking a lesson
from the multihued meanings of thumri gayaki, I proceeded
to encourage the children to see the song as a description
of Mother Earth rather than Motherland—everyone's earth,
rather than specifically the soil of the Indian nation, or a
religious symbol. This Mataram, this Mother, is everyone's
earth, and yet 'belongs' to no one—autonomous, one in
herself. And indeed the first verse of the song makes no
mention of any one geographical or political territory, makes
no mention of enemies who will be slain by the Motherland.
It can be heard, simply, as a song in praise of what
e.e. cummings has called our 'sweet spontaneous earth'. I
realize this does not solve the deep-rooted problems at the
heart of the controversy, the mischievous attempts by various
groups to foment trouble and divisiveness through this song.
Yet, perhaps, the discussion helped clear something—that
the earth belongs to us all, that the earth is beautiful and
deserving of our respect, and that hardened identities of

nation, religion and so on are in the end mere (if problematic) illusions. And so the children and I sing and talk about the Earth, our mother. I tell them of cummings's poem and of another by Kathleen Raine that speaks of 'one green leaf that opens for the heart the shelter of a great forest'. We speak of 'polluted tide', of 'desecrated earth, destroyed' and of our responsibility, each one of us to care for and love and protect this earth-mother. We sing songs about rivers and flowers and fields, and then in the light of this, the children sing '*Vande Mataram*' again and it takes on another meaning.

I remember again Nainaji's '*Vande Mataram*' and wonder how she would have responded. I remember her telling me about old singers who would deflect a difficult situation without causing offence, yet making clear their own autonomy, and I thank her for her teachings and hope that I have been able to live out at least a little of what she taught me.

And how could Nainaji not have met Gandhi? As a child of eight or nine, she had gone up to him and asked why he had such large ears. He had laughed and said he needed big ears to be able to hear the problems and sorrows of all the people of India.

The child who asked that question—was she Nilina or Sadhona?

When Nainaji tells me this story, the child is herself. Another time, in an article she has written in the 1970s about 'my beloved Mejdi', I read this same story. And here the child is Sadhona. I wonder about that mix-up of identities. Is it just an accident, a lapse of memory? Or does that blurring mean something else? Nilina and Sadhona—are they two people, or one, or many more than two?

-≫≫-≪≪-

Saral Babu and Nellie had five children—three girls and two boys. Nainaji was the fourth child, and the youngest of the daughters. The pattern of their lives was such that the brothers and sisters spent much of their time apart, in separate worlds. It was therefore with her sisters that she had her closest ties. So close were these three sisters—Benita, Sadhona and Nilina—that they were often referred to as a single being; the Besani sisters. They were a talented lot. Nilina was musical, Benita found expression in writing— plays, poetry, stories, and later founded and edited a magazine for women called *Gourika*. Sadhona, exquisitely beautiful, grew up to be a gifted dancer and actress, making a runaway marriage at the age of fifteen with the theatre and film director Madhu Bose. Benita married while Nilina was still a child, and moved to far-off Rangamati, now in Bangladesh. So it was with her Mejdi, Sadhona, that little Nilina had her closest ties. Nilina adored her vivacious, effervescent sister.

Though Sadhona died several years ago, in 1973, she seems to live on in Nainaji's life. Rarely can Nainaji tell me about herself or her childhood, rarely can she talk about music, dance, theatre or film without referring to Sadhona Bose. Mejdi's photograph greets you as you enter Nainaji's house. An extraordinarily beautiful woman, she looks out of the picture frame with a sidelong glance, pallu demurely over her head. Her lovely fingers hold the pallu in what can only be an exquisite dance mudra. There is mischief in her eyes; she seems about to break into song, or laughter. She holds my gaze as she has held Nainaji's devoted attention all these years. Nainaji's papers are full of old clippings from newspapers of the 1930s and 40s, hailing the beautiful young dancer or acclaiming her performances in plays and films such as *Ali Baba* and *Rajnartaki*. Mother, aunts, sisters—all seem to be present when Nainaji speaks, but none so clearly and palpably as Sadhona. It is almost as if she is, has never ceased to be, a part of Nainaji's own being. There is an almost fairytale-like quality to their relationship.

As she speaks, I recognize echoes from my own life, of my own relationships with my sisters. Are these events that she recounts to me 'real' or are they the working out of a mythic motif in the life of every woman? Do these events really happen in that way, or do they shape themselves as they are told and heard? Or are they actually the signposts, markers of our lives, patterns that occur like those on a snake's skin, and that we, half-dreaming, choose to weave into the tapestries of our stories?

What is it I wonder, that is so special about the relationship between sisters? Sadhona and Nilina; Snow White and Rose Red; my sister and I. How different are these relationships, how differently perceived, articulated and inscribed from the more structured relationships between men—brothers, fathers and sons—or even between mothers and their children! There is that magical bond between sisters—the sharing of secrets, nurturing each other, telling stories, protecting the younger, adoring the elder, caring for each other even when separated by the endless, non-traversable roads from one sister's sasural to the other's. Every woman speaks of her sister with a special warmth in her voice, the shared pranks of childhood, the sadness at separations, the special joy at the birth of a sister's child. To whom does one turn when distressed, but to one's sister? With whom else does one share one's deepest joy?

⇛⠀⋘

When Nainaji speaks about Mejdi, my own sisters are there with me. My sister is my child, my mother, my dearest friend, my greatest rival. My sister is the person most like myself; my sister is yet so indubitably, unforgivably other: me and not-me. I am like my sister, yet I can never be like her. In my sister's eyes I see myself as loving and lovable, as loved; her eyes are a mirror to my deepest anxieties and fears. My sister is my other face; my sister's life is the road not taken. My sister and I are two banks of a river; our lives run eternally parallel. Between myself and this beloved other is only a sparkling, flowing boundary that both separates and unites us.

And yet, nowhere is this relationship named, mythologized, given a formal place. No rituals celebrate the love that sisters share. No days are set apart for sisters to fast for each other's long life and well-being. Ever present, the surest thing in a woman's world, a sister's love remains unnamed, as elusive, yet as integral to her life as the fragrance of flowers on the breeze.

Once upon a time, I could write, there were two sisters, Sadhona and Nilina … both beautiful and talented and charming. Both grew up and went their very different ways…

It seems to me as if each explored for the other the path that her sister had not taken. Like a meteor, Sadhona shot to fame by the age of fourteen with her dancing, and her role as Marjina in *Ali Baba*. Sadhona's was a turbulent life. There was her marriage, first controversial, then difficult, with the film and theatre director Modhu Bose. She travelled all over India dancing and acting, and received the adulation of her audiences. But problems overtook her and proved too much for her. Unable to cope with her unhappiness she fell chronically ill and died, lonely and unhappy. Nilina was then in her fifties, and well into her own career. She had had her share of tragedy, including watching her beloved Mejdi give in to despair and then to death. But she was to write her own story very differently.

In the eternity of childhood, however, all that was hidden. Nilina's world was safe and secure, and Mejdi was her dearest friend forever. The greatest bond between them was a shared love of music, dance and theatre. The two girls would often perform in amateur theatre, and Nilina also played a small part, that of Sakina, in *Ali Baba*. Once, when they were dancing, Anna Pavlova was present in the audience. Nainaji tells me that Pavlova was so charmed, she asked to be allowed to take the girls back with her to Russia for intensive training in dance. The Sens refused, much to the girls' chagrin. For the Sens, a profession as a performing artiste was out of the question.

Sadhona was more extroverted than the placid Nilina, but they both knew they were different from other girls. 'We are truly mad!' they would giggle after a flight of daydreaming or a bit of mischief. Their mother was to explain, half ruefully, half laughingly, the reason behind Sadhona's passion for dance and theatre: The house adjoining Lily Cottage had belonged to a wealthy merchant who, each night, would organize mehfils of the singer Srijan Bai. Sadhona must have heard and internalized Srijan Bai's music while still in her mother's womb. How else to explain Sadhona's behaviour!

–≫ ≪–

Despite the ambivalent attitude towards the professional stage, inherited from Keshub Chandra Sen and the spirit of the time, the young men of the Sen family continued to frequent the theatre and even befriend actresses. That is how the famous actresses and singers Kananbala, Regina, Angurbala entered, if obliquely, the lives of the Sen girls.

'Panchu Kaka, my father's cousin took me to the theatre once. I was very young then, only eight or nine. I was overjoyed at the treat; in those days theatre was full of song and dance, and I loved music. The play starred Angurbala, a famous singer and actress of those days. I sat enthralled—such a beautiful woman, such wonderful singing!'

Later, as they went home, Panchu Kaka asked his niece if she had liked the play, and what she had thought of Angurbala. Laughing at the child's enthusiastic response, he then asked her if she would like to meet Angurbala one day. Wide-eyed with excitement, the little girl pleaded, 'Yes, oh yes, please!'

Of course, it had to be a secret from her parents. While it was customary for elite and wealthy young men to visit singers and actresses, it was certainly not considered proper for a little girl to be taken to meet one of them at her salon.

'One evening Panchu Kaka came to take me out for a drive. We had already planned that we would actually go to Angurbala's house in Masjid Bari. I had dressed with care, wearing my best blue organdie frock. My hair was combed into ringlets and since this was a very special occasion, I had dusted my face liberally with powder.'

She turns to me laughing. 'Would you believe it, in those days we used talcum powder on our faces! Then I was ready to go. I could barely contain my excitement. The ride in the Victoria seemed interminable, but at last, we were there!'

Angurbala, the star of Minerva Theatres, like many of the actresses of those days, came from the community of professional singing women. She had shot into prominence in 1925 with her role as Vivek in *Atmadarshan*, and was now one of Calcutta's most popular actresses. She was considered one of the finest singers of Bengali theatre, of All India Radio, Calcutta, and of the gramophone companies. She and her sister, Bedaani Sundari Bai were famous for their good looks.

'Angurbala was sitting in a large, beautiful room on a white chandni chadar. There were bolsters on the floor, and near her, lay a silver paandaan. On the walls hung full-length mirrors with intricately carved silver frames. She was beautiful and gracious, everything I had imagined her to be. Panchu Kaka, whom she seemed to know well, had apparently told her he would be bringing me to meet her. She welcomed me affectionately and graciously. She sat me on her lap, stroked my cheeks and then fed me a rasgolla. She asked me if I liked music, and if I would sing for her. I loved singing, and needed no second bidding.'

I look at Nainaji and now I see a little girl in a blue organdie dress, singing for the great Angurbala. I see Angurbala listening gravely, carefully. She listens to the child as if she, too, were an artiste, not just a little girl in a blue organdie frock with too much talcum powder on her face. The song ends, and Angurbala hugs and blesses the child.

'Then,' says Nainaji, 'I asked her to sing for me and—she was so gracious—she did! I went home in a daze, scarcely believing that this strange, wonderful experience was true. It wasn't a dream. Clutched tight in my fist was a scrap of paper with Angurbala's telephone number. After all these years, I still remember it—3226 Burra Bazar—and the memory of her promise that I could speak to her on the telephone whenever I wished and that she would sing for me if I did. I went through the next few days hugging my secret to myself.'

But what good is a secret if it can't be shared? And whom else to share it with but Mejdi? Mejdi—older, more mischievous, more knowing of the world outside Lily Cottage—Mejdi understood the need for total secrecy.

The two girls would ring up Angurbala, and as promised, she would sing to them over the telephone. Nainaji described to Mejdi the beautiful house at Masjid Bari and the girls would spin dreams of growing up to be famous singers and actresses: 'We imagined we would live in big houses in Masjid Bari and people would come to our mehfils to hear us sing.' She laughs, and, a little embarrassed, says, 'We didn't know what it meant to be a professional singer, a baiji.'

How did her parents find out about this escapade? Nainaji doesn't know. But murder will out, and one day, the secret was discovered. Panchu Kaka was, for a long while, prohibited from entering the house; the girls were severely punished.

'But I never forgot Angurbala. Years later, sometime in the 1960s, Angurbala came to sing in Delhi at the Kali Bari Puja celebrations. I went to hear her. She was old now, her beauty had faded, her voice was a dim memory of its former glory, but that andaz, that pukar…! I went backstage to meet her after the programme. Would she remember me? I had met her just once, nearly fifty years ago. I said to her, "You may not remember me. I am Nilina Sen."

'She jumped up and hugged me. There were tears in her eyes. She stroked my cheeks and asked after Panchu Kaka—long dead by then—and, smiling through her tears she said: "I've sung for you. Will you sing for me now?"'

4

The Pleasures of Silence

In the years between those two meetings, Nainaji was married and had had four children. The Mejdi of her childhood had changed from a beautiful, laughter-loving girl to an ailing, unhappy woman, while Nainaji herself had been suddenly and tragically widowed. Shifting to Delhi from Rajanagar, she had come back to music, learning first from Ghulam Sabir Khan Ambalewale, then from Mushtaq Hussain Khan, and finally coming under the influence of Rasoolan Bai. She had begun singing over the radio, changing her name from Nilina Ripjit Singh to Naina Devi, to conceal her identity at a time when singing, especially thumri and ghazal, was considered taboo for 'respectable' women. She had worked as the director of the newly established College of Hindustani Music and Dance that is now known as the Shriram Bharatiya Kala Kendra. She had gone on to become programme director at All India Radio and, later, at Doordarshan. In 1961 she had founded, along with some other musicians and musicologists, a cultural organization, Raag Rang, which organized many memorable mehfils. She was also to work out a housing programme for artistes and to convert her own home into a performance space, a home for travelling artistes, and a refuge for them when they were old and ill and in need of help. Awards would come her way too—the Padma Shri in 1974, and many others—recognizing her great contribution to music and culture.

Nainaji was married in 1935 to Rajkumar Ripjit Singh, the youngest son of Raja Charanjit Singh of the royal family of Kapurthala. He was several years older than her, a mature twenty-seven to her girlish seventeen. The marriage brought a great change in her life, involving a move from Bengal and life at Lily Cottage, to far-off Punjab and western UP. Home was now Ripjit Singh's estate in Rajanagar, near Shahjahanpur, with frequent visits to their other houses in Delhi, Jalandhar and Shimla.

A nursery rhyme of her childhood, sung to her by her ayah, resonated with this great change in her life— 'Punjabi boli bolo, Bangali meri jaan': Speak Punjabi then, little Bengali darling! She sings it now, a simple little tune, and says, 'I didn't know then that it would come true for me.'

-≫≪-

I often wonder about this marriage. How did it come about? When I ask her, she brushes the question away. I persist with my questioning: 'How did your parents arrange your marriage so far away, into a family so different from their own? How did your parents decide to marry you off when you were so young?'

She slips out of the net of my questions, so smoothly, so gracefully that I am barely aware of it. In retrospect I see the evasion, the chori, and I remember a story she once told me:

'Isharat Bai was dancing. It was in Rajanagar, and I was watching from behind my chilman. A man, one of the audience, reached out and grabbed her hand. Without

breaking the laya, the rhythm of her movements, Isharat
Bai gently freed her hand. It was done so gracefully no one
would have guessed it was not part of the dance. Smiling a
little, charming as ever, she said in the voice of the nayika of
so many thumris, gently reproachful "Zyadti mat keejiye—
Please! Not so impetuous!"'

It is Rena who tells me. Rena is Nainaji's daughter, her
second child, Billy didi to me. She is an interior designer,
tall and elegant, and lived at that time in a white-and-silver
flat in Sunder Nagar, close to Nainaji's own Kaka Nagar
government accommodation.

Ripjit Singh was visiting Calcutta with his sister, Pamela,
to shop for her wedding trousseau. They had called on the
Sens. Ripjit Singh's curiosity about the Sens had already been
aroused by Pamela's fiancé who had written to him urging him
to visit the Sens and mentioning a daughter—'no paragon of
beauty, but what a voice!' (He was wrong, I think—she is a
paragon of beauty too!) And so Ripjit Singh had called on
the Sens, had seen the young Nilina, had heard her sing, and
had fallen promptly and irrevocably in love. He had refused
to leave Calcutta till the Sens agreed to a marriage, and had
written to his father informing him of his decision. Billy didi
says, 'Papaji, my grandfather, didn't wholly approve of the idea
of a bride from so distant a place. But finally, acknowledging
defeat to his adamant son, he wrote to him: "I give you my
consent, not my blessings..."'

Nainaji had said once, 'My parents agreed because they
wanted me to settle down; I was getting too deeply into
music for comfort...' Perhaps Nellie was thinking of Sadhona.
Perhaps, she wanted to protect this youngest daughter from
the choices Sadhona had made, choices that would lead to
such tragic consequences for her.

Billy didi says, 'I think my grandparents saw how much Daddy loved my mother. And then there was the fact that he was a son of the royal family of Kapurthala. Maybe they thought Mummy would be happy, comfortable and secure. Kapurthala, small though it was, was nevertheless one of the richest and most glamorous of the princely states. And for Didima and my Nana, though they were not poor, life had not been very easy. I think they agreed because it seemed to be the best of all possible marriages—a wealthy prince, and a man who loved Mummy for herself.'

In my mind, her story resonates with echoes of the Cooch Behar marriage. This marriage of a Sen daughter to a prince is, after all, not so different. Was this then an accepted, if unarticulated pattern in the Sen family? Was this why Sadhona's was such a controversial marriage? Benita had married the Raja of the Chakmas. Nilina became a young Rani of the Kapurthala rajwada. But Sadhona, irrepressible, unpredictable—had she followed just her heart when she married a fellow artiste, when she tried, unconsciously perhaps, to close the gap between wife and performer, between wife and woman?

If I had asked Sadhona about her life, where the role of wife did not preclude that of artiste, how would she have answered? If I had asked her about Nilina's life what would she have said? Did Sadhona consciously articulate her brave decision, or did she just live it because that was her given life? Like many women before and after her, who insist on the full coat, not just a patch, life was hard on Sadhona. She suffered greatly; she died a broken, unhappy woman. Sometimes in those last days she would be angry with her sister Nilina, whose life, hard though it was, seemed well-ordered and peaceful compared to the turbulence of Sadhona's.

I feel her pain, her anger, her loneliness. Suddenly I wish
that I had known this other brave, charming, unhappy, angry
sister who tried to write for herself a story for which there
were still no words. I want to tell her that her life is being
heard too, that someone believes in her choices—that in the
end, her life was the right life, the best life for her. She need
have no regrets.

⇒⟫ ⟪⟸

Raja Charanjit Singh's withheld blessings notwithstanding
Nilina and Ripjit's wedding was a grand affair, and the guest
list a veritable who's who of India's elite. But what Nainaji
remembers about it was that Pandit Ram Chatur Malik
was invited to sing at the celebrations. Among the people
who blessed the young bride were Prince Akram Hussain
and Prince Sulaiman Qadr, sons of Wajid Ali Shah. They
were both close friends of Bade Sarkar—Nainaji's husband's
grandfather.

'Sulaiman Qadr and Bade Sarkar had exchanged turbans;
they were as close as brothers. After 1856 when the British
annexed Lucknow, Sulaiman Qadr would spend six months
of each year in Awadh and the other six with our family.
Prince Akram Hussain also used to spend long periods with
us. He would tell me many stories about the fabulous court
of Wajid Ali Shah and about the music, dance and drama
that used to take place there.'

All this would find expression later in the many ballets
and 'musical extravaganzas' she would organize through the
Bharatiya Kala Kendra or through Raag Rang—*Shaan-e-Awadh,
Dalia, Inder Sabha, Rang Basanti, Sawan Bhadon*—and in
the décor and setting for Raag Rang's Naaz-o-ada mehfils
devoted to performances of thumri, ghazal and kathak.

Other people now entered her life in place of the social reformers and singers of her childhood. She tells me, 'I was busy being hostess at my father-in-law's many banquets.' She slipped easily into her new role, dealing faultlessly with the labyrinth of protocol, the arsenals of cutlery that such a role entailed. 'Viceroys, nawabs, maharajas, civil servants—I met so many people then.'

Princess Sita Devi of Kapurthala, an aunt by marriage, tells me: 'I remember the first time I saw her. She had come to Kapurthala. Of course, we had all heard about her: how pretty she was and what a sweet voice she had. She came to meet me with her sister-in-law, Pamela, her baby daughter in her arms. We all loved her. She was so sweet and gentle. She was the ideal daughter-in-law.'

Billy didi says, 'She won everyone over. She fitted in beautifully.'

As I remember, as I write, I discover that those years seem telescoped into a few brief sentences. I know little about her life as a married woman. She tells me so little. And I realize today that I really don't need to know. The Naina Devi who did not sing and teach is, for me, another person, one with whom I have little connection, except to wonder at her complete acceptance, then and later, of those silent years.

She would speak to me more about the trauma of being widowed, and of the strange way in which the very moment of her greatest grief became the turning point in her life. 'But for that tragedy,' she would often say, 'I would never have become a singer.'

When she spoke at all about those years of her life as a daughter-in-law of the royal family of Kapurthala, she spoke of herself just so, as the daughter-in-law of a rajwada, as the gracious hostess. And even when others tell me about those years, I hear about her sweetness and grace, what a charming hostess she was and how beautifully she fitted in with the lifestyle of Kapurthala.

But she often speaks of the times when she was able to hear music—about Benazir Bai, Isharat Bai and many others—and the stories she tells are rich with detail. Sometimes she tells about the times when she hummed and sang as she and her husband and their friends drove out on picnics.

It seems to me that she is reliving those moments, those cherished tenuous connections with music, as she teaches me a ghazal one day. 'Qateel Shifai wrote this for me,' she says:

> Jo chaahte ho, so kehte ho
> Chup rahne ki lazzat kya jano
> Ye raaz-e-mohabbat hai pyaare,
> Tum raaz-e-mohabbat kya jano.

> You say what you will, carelessly.
> What do you know of the taste, the pleasures of
> silence.
> This silence that is the secret of love;
> What do you know of this secret?

Whose silence, I wonder? Was Qateel making a point here when he spoke of silence and careless speech? I don't ask and Nainaji doesn't speak further. Perhaps, we both prefer the pleasures of silence. But for me this ghazal and the raaz-e-mohabbat, the love it speaks of, opens up to many, many meanings.

'We were in Shimla, sitting in the garden of our house, Chapslee, when Qateel wrote these verses,' Nainaji says. 'He wrote them for me.' I sing them then with this new knowledge of her silence, her masking speech, and Qateel's relentless hearing.

She talks often about Chapslee, the family home in Shimla. She tells me that the house was once owned by the British, and that it was here that Lord Auckland signed the treaty after the devastating Afghan War. Chapslee is now a heritage hotel run by the present owner, Ratanjit Singh, Nainaji's son. Ratanjit Singh has taken care to maintain the flavour of the house with its different layers of history—both of the British and of Indian royalty.

She tells me about times spent in Shimla, of the beauty of the mountains, of the sparkling life of the elite holiday resort, about the Mall and the Gaiety Theatre.

She tells me of the time she and her husband once drove from Delhi to Shimla: 'I sang all the way in the car. I don't know how the time went by.'

Then one day in the present that I share with her, invited to sing at a private concert at what is now 20 Akbar Road in Delhi, she tells me as we sit down and start tuning the tanpuras, that as a married woman she had lived in this very house, sat in this very room. She points to where once there had been a picture on a wall, where once a chandelier had hung from the roof; she looks out to where there had once been a rose garden.

The house is different now. Someone else lives here, and the walls, the ceiling, the gardens bear the stamp of this new owner's life. But as she speaks, the solid walls of the house become transparent; they reveal that other house, the house of her memory. An elaborately laid dinner table, crisp white table linen, an elegant hostess and her splendid guests. Which house is this in which she sits now and sings? It seems so very strange that she should be singing here, in this very space where once she would only have listened, hidden by a chilman, to other singers.

-»> «<-

The paucity of the information she gives me makes me wonder. Did she not want to speak, or did she think that in this relationship with me, a younger woman, coincidentally, and strangely, retracing her own steps, those years were of less consequence than the years of preparation and then the years of doing? The years of her marriage were happy years. Of that I have no doubt. But in the story of her life as I think she wanted me to hear it, were they years to be glossed over quickly; compressed into brief statements?

It is from the Begum of Rampur that I hear another story—about Nainaji singing in Rampur. When I ask Nainaji about it, she smiles and says, 'That was not in public. I never sang in public in Rampur. The Nawab Saheb and the Begum Saheba were always conscious of and respected the fact that I was the daughter-in-law of the royal state of Kapurthala.'

I hear this charming story when one morning Nainaji and I set out, armed with a tape recorder, to meet her friend the Begum Saheba of Rampur. Years ago, the Begum Saheba had pointed out to a little girl, each wonderful performer at a naach in a house called Emerald Bower. That little girl, quite grown up now, wants Begum Saheba to speak, to reminisce about the cultural life of Rampur and tell her again about all that she has seen and heard.

It proves to be a magical morning. Begum Saheba tells us about Wazir Khan, Achhan Maharaj and Lachhu Maharaj. She describes performances by Nanua Jan and Bachua Jan. She brings alive memories of the famous Gauhar Jan, an accomplished artiste, who was fluent in a dozen or more

languages. About her, Begum Saheba said, 'People paid
fortunes just for the privilege of conversing with her. She was
'kept' by no man. Instead, the world danced to her tune.'
Begum Saheba recalls witnessing the famous mor paran,
dance of the peacock: 'Flour was brought and spread on the
floor. Then Lachhu Maharaj began to dance the mor paran.
When the paran was over, when the dancer executed the last
swirl and stood still, so we knew he was only a man, and not,
as it had seemed, a peacock, I looked down at the floor. And
indeed, the flour had been transformed by the movements of
his feet into a resplendent dancing peacock.'

And then, suddenly she adds, 'And I remember you, Rani.
I remember you, singing, and Nawab Saheb and I listening
to you. I remember Mushtaq Hussain Khan sitting by you,
patting your back and encouraging you—"jeeti raho beti!"'

'I wasn't singing professionally then,' Nainaji tells me later.
'That was long before I started learning from Khan Saheb.
I never sang in public in Rampur. For the Nawab and the
Begum, I was always, first and foremost, the daughter-in-law
of a rajwada whose dignity had to be maintained by keeping
to certain rules.'

Those were happy years. And yet, there was an emptiness.
There was no music.

→≫ ≪←

There was no music except for what she heard in small,
informal mehfils, or the mujras she would witness from
behind her chilman. There was no singing except for the
songs sung informally at parties, at the request of friends.
'People would ask me to sing a ghazal and I would do so
immediately, without any accompaniment.' Perhaps she was
barely aware of this absence. After all, music as a profession

was not really an option available to women like her. She
never speaks of it thus.

And yet, surely there must have been some sense of loss?
I wonder about this when she tells me, one day, about Zohra
Begum. 'Someone in the family had married a tawaif. The
marriage had understandably caused a scandal; everyone
had been, and still was most upset by it. No one spoke to
Zohra Begum if they could help it. She was shunned and
ostracized, never allowed to forget who she was. I felt
sorry for her, alone amid hostile in-laws. And I felt sorry
for her, especially, because she had given up the life of an
artiste—the absorption in riyaz, the performances, singing,
dancing, basking in the admiration and the gifts that men
laid at her feet. She had given up all that, exchanging it for the
stolid security of marriage. I realized that like so many other
tawaifs she too was aware of the fleeting nature of the good
times she enjoyed as a singer. An artiste's life is short—old
age, illness, childbirth can finish her career completely. And
who is there in the bad times to care for the tawaif, a woman
who has given her youth to pleasing others? I understood
why she had married, why she had made this choice.'

As Nainaji speaks, I remember a character from a childhood
story, Anderson's mermaid, who chose to exchange her fish's
tail for legs, and a human soul, but each step she took, cut
through her like knives and she lost the power to speak.

Zohra Begum lost the power to speak or sing, to look at
anyone else's face, to be looked at. In exchange for the security
and respectability of marriage, she became a pale ghost
hovering between two worlds, a creature alone, belonging
nowhere. Only the new young Bengali bride visited her,
spoke to her, understood the pain of her two lives, the pain
of her choice.

The years went by. Four children were born, two girls and two boys. Then in 1946, in Lucknow, Nainaji unexpectedly met an old friend from the past. Sunil Bose was a gurubhai, a fellow student of Girija Babu's. A fine, sensitive singer, he had joined All India Radio and was working in Lucknow. The two were overjoyed at meeting each other after so many years, and Nainaji and her husband became frequent visitors at Sunil-da's home, where he would insist that Nainaji sing. Nainaji's eyes mist over as she tells how, strangely, a few months before he died, her husband, inspired perhaps by Sunil-da's enthusiasm, encouraged her to record some dadras and ghazals. And so in 1948, in Lucknow, she cut her first record with the Columbia Record Company. She recorded two dadras, '*Gori tore nainva ke baan*' and '*Bol more raja*', taught to her so many years before by Girija Babu. 'I think my husband must have had a premonition of his death. Perhaps he saw, unconsciously, the course my life would take, and he was preparing me for that.'

He died suddenly. He had been ill and Nainaji had gone with him to Calcutta where he was being treated by their family physician, Dr B.C. Roy. His health improved and the couple celebrated, on 14 August 1949, their fourteenth wedding anniversary in Calcutta. The very next day there was a message from Nainaji's father-in-law, asking them to return immediately to Shimla. It was decided that Nainaji would travel back to Shimla but her husband would stay on in Calcutta for a few more days. He had recovered though; there was no cause for worry. As she left Calcutta with her youngest child, four-year-old Kenny (Karanjit Singh), Nainaji said to her husband, 'After so many years we are again together in Calcutta on our wedding day. At that time too, after the wedding, we had gone to Shimla. It is all exactly as it was so many years ago, only this time I am going back to Shimla alone.'

She turns to me: 'How strange it is, the way fate puts words into our mouths. I had no idea what was going to happen, yet what I had said came true. That was the last time I saw my husband. I went to Shimla alone. And after that, I made all journeys alone. His blood pressure rose suddenly, and fatally. Before anything could be done, he had died....

'Early that same morning in Shimla, I was woken up by Kenny. He was saying, urgently, "Mummy, bolo Radhe-Shyam, bolo Sita-Ram!" (Say Radhe-Shyam, say Sita-Ram). I felt strangely unnerved when I heard him. I had a sense that something was wrong. A few hours later, I received a telegram summoning me back to Calcutta; it said my husband was ill. I wasn't told that he was already dead. I drove down to Delhi and then flew to Calcutta. As I came up to my brother's house where my husband was staying, I wondered at the number of cars at the gate and in the drive. Why have so many people come to see my husband when he's ill? I thought to myself. He should be allowed to rest. As I entered the house and my brother came up to me, I saw his bare feet. Then I knew that my husband was dead.'

Life was very difficult. She tells me of the hardships she had to face. The funeral over, she went back to Rajanagar, but family jealousies, rivalries and litigations now raised their ugly heads. 'I was all alone in Rajanagar, and afraid. In those days, the area was dacoit-infested and quite unsafe. I couldn't count on help from my in-laws. For some reason many of them had turned against me.'

It is, of course, a familiar pattern—the young widow, isolated, far away from her childhood home, suddenly an outsider in the home of her husband. Perhaps, this was when awareness dawned that we belong nowhere, are related to no one. And out of this terrible emptiness perhaps, also came the sureness, the centredness that is the mark of an artiste.

I remember her saying to me once, 'An artist can love no-one, only his art.' Strangely, almost contrarily, she had just been telling me about the passionate love affair of the nineteenth-century poet Daag Dehlavi and the beautiful singer and poet Hijaab. She had been teaching me a ghazal of Daag's and had spoken of the transparent simplicity of his poetry, about Daag's life and his meeting with Hijaab at Rampur's Benazir Ka Mela in the monsoon month of Sawan.

'An artiste can love no one, only his art', Nainaji tells me this. It seems almost like a piece of advice, a naseehat, something I must understand and live by. And yet at other times she has said, equally seriously, 'You cannot sing thumri unless you first learn to love—recklessly, totally...'

How do I understand these two seemingly opposed statements? Thinking about this, I realize that she was not speaking of the ability to love, to feel, to relate to another, but more, of what often happens in the name of love—of the abdicating of one's priorities, one's own life, and the confounding of the centre of one's being towards maintaining the social facade that we sometimes mistake for 'love'.

Perhaps it was this centre that she touched in her loneliness and fear. Perhaps she came to the realization that for her, all roles, all loves came after what must then have been dimly perceived as her primary commitment to herself as an artiste. Perhaps she realized that relationships with others—with parents, spouse, friends, even with one's children—are in some fashion external to one's self, are social, are 'made' relationships as A K Ramanujan has called them. But the relationship to one's self, to the core of one's being, a relationship that then flows forth as love of others, as music and poetry and art—perhaps she was telling me—this was real, central, this was non-negotiable.

This question—how to reconcile her seemingly contradictory statements—has stayed with me and haunts me even today. It seems to me that the answer lies in discovering the strength and courage to live a razor-edged life: to be deeply loving, to be intensely vulnerable and open to life with all its delights and terrors, and simultaneously, to be somehow 'away' from it all, to be unshakeable, rooted in the unnameable, indescribable vastness of my miniscule, flawed being. Nainaji's words echo in my heart, and I hear her tell me to live fully, to drink deeply of all experiences, yet to remain untouched in some essential way by any of them; to move and change every minute, yet remain still and unchanging, to love deeply, yet not barter my self away for love.

It seems to me that what Nainaji had hinted at is an unshakeable, unimpeachable centredness, a selfsuffiency, a completeness that is what the Viveka Chudamani speaks of:

> *Purnam ada purnam idam*
> *Purnaat purnamaduchyate*
> *Purnasya purnamadaya*
> *Purnameva vasishyate*

> That is complete, this is complete
> Add to completeness, it is still complete
> Remove from it, and that is complete
> What remains is still complete.

It seems to me, too, that this centredness in the self is so different from self-centredness, self-absorbtion, selfishness. In the early 1980s, feminists, mainly in the West, grappling with issues of women and art had urged women, especially women artists, to be a little 'selfish', to 'claim' and 'defend' their time and space from the demands made on them by patriarchal societies and their stereotypical roles. While this made considerable sense to me, and indeed was a source of great inspiration, something troubled me. These words— 'claim', 'defend', 'selfish'—they seem to have resonances of the adversarial; they pit us (in this case, women) against someone or something from whom/which we have to strain and struggle to wrest time and space, the right to be. But Nainaji's words pointed me in another direction: the quality of centredness that her words exhort me to realize is a state that is inclusive, non-oppositional, yet uncompromising for all that.

I hear Nainaji's voice again, as I write this; I hear her laughter as she speaks of this most grave and significant matter. She seems to be telling me to walk this tightrope, perform this balancing act between a joyous and deeply loving engagement with the world, and a complete retreat into the silence and stillness of one's being. As I write, fragments of ghazals she has taught me, of poems and sutras I have read, flit through my mind.

So does the Buddhist sutra advise:

> As in the ocean's midmost depths, no wave is born,
> but all is still

So let the monk be still, be motionless and nowhere
should he swell.

Or Faiz's ironic lines that echo for me what Nainaji implies
when she speaks of the way we surrender the truth of our
selves to the clamour of social norms. Is this 'another' that
he speaks of, or our own selves when he says:

> Duniya ne teri yaad se begaana kar diya
> Tujhse bhi dil-fareb hain gham rozgaar ke,

> The business of living estranges me from your memory
> More faithless, more deceitful than you, the cares of
> this life…!

Or Siraj Arangabadi's exquisite ghazal that seems to say
it all:

> Khabar-e tahaiyur-e ishq sun, na junoon raha, na
> pari rahi
> Na to tu raha, na to main raha, jo rahi so bekhabari
> rahi.
> Chali simt-e ghaib se ik hava, ke chaman zahoor ka
> jal gaya
> Magar ek shakh-e nihaal-e gham jise dil kaho so hari
> rahi.

> Listen to this tale of a devastating love, where
> neither love nor the object of love remained
> I was not I, nor were you, you. All that remained
> was an obliviousness.
> From some unknowable vastness blew a wind that
> burnt the world-garden
> Yet, one vulnerable branch—call it the heart—
> stayed fresh and green.

The love that Siraj speaks of, that Nainaji tells me about,
is far beyond the sentimental, far beyond the romantic. It

seems to me that there is no 'other' here, and yet all others are brought into the vastness of its embrace. Such a love, Siraj tells us, is possible only when one takes on the eternal 'burning'—a brilliant blaze that gives light and warmth, but that also devastates and destroys the safeness of the known world, one's cherished and petty notions of oneself and one's life; it empties us of all sense of self, of the distinction between 'me' and 'not me', between 'me' and 'the world', between 'self' and 'other'.

Now Nainaji's voice pulls me back to the room in her house in Kaka Nagar—to the sound of the fan whirring overhead, the gleam of the silver object d'art on the table that stands next to the divan on which we sit facing each other, her harmonium between us, as she punctuates her teaching of a dadra with these memories:

'I was so afraid, but equally, I was determined not to give in to fear and self-pity. I was determined to make a life for myself and my children, and to make it a good, happy life. My father had died earlier, but my mother was alive still. I could have gone to her in Calcutta. It would have been a good life in its own way. After all, so many women go back to their maika at such times. But something kept me from doing that. Something, some pride in myself, a belief that I would make a life for myself, a refusal to be frightened by the problems I was facing. Life had presented me with a challenge; I wasn't going to back down!'

But there was something else. After all, it is at times of crisis that one questions everything one has taken for granted. And perhaps, it is in attempting to answer and yet knowing there is no answer to the extraordinary mystery of life that we grow as individuals.

'I went through hell. You cannot imagine how terrible it was…'

As Nainaji describes to me the loneliness, misunderstandings and isolation of those years, I see her, still so very young, adrift midstream, the course of life's journey all upset. Like many women in such situations she turned to service and social work. 'I had two ambitions as a child—to sing well and to be a doctor. I don't know how it happened but I began to give medicines to the villagers,' she says. Yet as she speaks, I know that it was only a matter of time before she saw clearly that this was not her chosen path.

She didn't know that then; only that living a life of lonely grieving in a village in UP, doling out medicines to grateful villagers was not her life. So one day, persuaded by a friend, she appeared for an audition at All India Radio, Delhi, under the name of Naina Devi. 'I would travel from Rajanagar to Delhi for recordings. No one in AIR knew who I was.'

This first small act led to others that would change her life completely.

It began with despair: 'I couldn't take it any more—the whispers, the rivalries, the litigation…' all the petty and not so petty cruelties, that so many women suffer, their stories surprisingly similar in the litany of daily abuse. 'I wanted nothing more than to get away from it all and make a new life for myself.'

She severed the last remaining tie with her old life. She donated three hundred acres of agricultural land in Rajanagar to the area's landless peasants. Three of her children were already in boarding schools. Now Kenny, the youngest was also sent to one. Then, she moved to Delhi.

⇒⇒⇒ ⇐⇐⇐

Sumitra Charat Ram had just set up the College of Hindustani Music and Dance. This institution is now known as the Shriram Bharatiya Kala Kendra. The College was envisaged as a place that would ensure the survival and continuity of the traditional arts in a changing world.

Mrs Charat Ram saw the college as an institution for the arts in the modern sense of the word, yet one where the traditional methods of transmission of knowledge would be followed, rather than those typical of a 'school' with fixed timings, a curriculum, and examinations. Traditionally, education in the arts had not been exclusive of education in life's values: the college sought to preserve this as the context in which the arts were handed down.

Nainaji became the first director of this institution. At that time, in the early 1950s, the college was housed in a flat on Pusa Road. Nainaji was also provided a home here. She began work in earnest, taking help from great artistes in this challenging task that had been entrusted to her.

It was a glittering galaxy that lived and taught at the college. Kathak maestros such as Shambhu Maharaj and Sunder Prasad and great musicians such as Hafiz Ali Khan, Mushtaq Hussain Khan, Vilayat Hussein Khan, the senior Dagar brothers, Wahid Hussain Khan, Siddheshwari Devi, Ishtiaq Hussain Khan, Habibuddin Khan and Purshottam Das. It meant a steady income for them at a time when the old avenues of patronage had changed, if not disappeared. It ensured the continuation of the guru-shishya tradition both in their own families and also through the dissemination of music and dance education to students not from the gharana's bloodline. Nainaji says, remembering fondly: 'Birju Maharaj and Amjad Ali Khan have grown up before my eyes. I have watched them learn and grow to be great artistes.'

Even today, when music has become so popular and patronage of the arts is again, though very differently, a mark of status, music remains a precarious profession. It fills the soul, not the stomach. It was to combat this that Nainaji worked along with Mrs Charat Ram to make the college and then the Kendra, a place that would provide financial and social security, time and opportunity for musicians and dancers to live, teach and perform, free of at least the worst of the pressures of survival in these hard times and thus keep their traditions alive.

When she talks about those days, it is about the work that she tells me—the dance-dramas, the artistes, the jokes and camaraderie. She speaks with warmth and admiration about Sumitra Charat Ram and their long association. 'If it had not been for Sumitraji, there may not have been a Naina Devi at all,' she says, acknowledging the fact that had it not been for a chance meeting when it was decided to entrust her with this herculean task, Nainaji herself may not have found the space and opportunity to flower nor to make her mark as an artiste, guru and patron. She would often recall her colleagues and the discussions, the freedom she found to experiment. It was at the Shriram Bharatiya Kala Kendra that she had the opportunity to meet and work with such people as Nirmala Joshi, whom she would often remember with great warmth, and who later became the first secretary of the newly set up Sangeet Natak Akademi. Nainaji tells me, 'It was the breadth of her vision and her nature, which was both scholarly and practical, that gave her an understanding of the problems involved in preserving the traditional arts in a rapidly changing society. She was a source of inspiration for me, a role model and a friend.'

Yet another person she would often speak of was Kapila Vatsyayan. She deemed her to be one of those rare people who combine a scholastic brilliance, a sensitivity to the nuances of art, and a holistic approach that linked the different art traditions with each other and with life.

And she would speak often of Sumitra Charat Ram, of her vision, of her dedication and determination to create an institution for the arts. 'Her contribution is immeasureable,' she would often say.

She tells me very little about herself—her inner thoughts and feelings. Is it that she forgets the hardship as indeed one always forgets the sharpness of pain? Or is it that she is unsure how to tell me about that other woman in that other time, who was still fashioning blind her life, who did not know how her story would go? Is it pride, an inability to expose those wounds to another? Or is it fear that the listener—or her own ear—might pick up the faintest texture of self-pity, of complaint?

It is Billy didi again who tells me, one oppressively hot evening as we sit in her beautiful room with its white painted furniture, drinking fragrant lemon tea. 'Two small rooms on Pusa Road. It was such a change from the French elegance of Kapurthala, from Chapslee's English charm, from the luxury and space of Rajanagar. I was eleven when Daddy died, fourteen when we moved to Delhi, old enough to understand and feel the change, but—I wonder how she did it—Mummy never let us feel anything was wrong. We never felt materially deprived, we never felt we had lost something. Only the security of Daddy's encircling arms. Mummy gave us everything, but no mother, however wonderful, can be a father as well. Daddy, warm, affectionate, was no more. That loss could never be made good.'

The face in the photographs in Nainaji's house springs to life as Billy didi speaks. I see fourteen-year-old Billy, on the threshold of womanhood, suddenly fatherless. Mummy's loving presence is a cocoon of security. But there is no father to guide her as she takes her first tentative steps into the world of adulthood and the world of adult love and relationships that come to her, once removed, through song and dance.

'Two small rooms … We had never even been out of the gate of the Rajanagar house on our own; we had travelled everywhere by car, we were sheltered, wrapped-in-cotton-wool kids. Yet it wasn't hard for us to shift gears and adjust to this new life; it was Mummy's attitude that made this possible. She never complained. And after all, remember, it must have been much, much harder on her.

'In the new flat, that was now our home, one room was used as a sitting room. The other was Mummy's bedroom that worked overtime as my room and our dining room as well. The divan opened out to become a bed. The cupboard was fitted out to double as a dressing table. We had so few things. I had just started college; June, my elder sister, Nilika, was married. My brothers, Reggie and Kenny were still at school. So it was I who experienced this change in her life with her. I had few clothes at an age when all girls like to dress up. Mummy had fewer still. But at that time it didn't seem important. Perhaps it was Mummy's ability to make a little go such a long way, to create a feeling of space, comfort and plenty out of so little.'

As she speaks I hear Nainaji's voice, as she once said to me, 'Wherever I've lived, whatever I've had, even if it's been very little, I've always lived comfortably—there's always been aaraam.'

Billy didi is thinking aloud: 'Was I just unable to appreciate the great difference? Was I insensitive, or was it

Lily Cottage, the Sen's family home

Saral Sen's prayer room

The Sens at a family picnic: Nainaji is the child on extreme left

The Sens at a family picnic

Nainaji's aunts: her father's sisters

Nainaji's maternal
grandmother
Mukta Devi

Nainaji's elder
brother Suneeth

Dancing in the
play 'Dalia'

With her sister
Sadhona Bose (right)
in the play 'Alibaba', as
Sakina

With Pandit
Girija Shankar Chakravarty and
two other students; Nainaji is
on the extreme right

With Prodeep, Sadhona
and parents

Nilina Ripjit Singh of Kapurthala

At a radio
recording,
mid 1950s

Ustad Ghulam Sabir Khan

In performance. Ustad
Ghulam Sabir Khan
on the sarangi

Rasoolan Bai

With Ustad Bade Ghulam
Ali Khan and Ustad
Mushtaq Hussain Khan

Tarikh-e-Thumri:
with Badi Moti Bai,
Siddheshwari Devi
and Rasoolan Bai

Tarikh-e-Kathak:
with Birju Maharaj
and Roshan Kumari

With Raichand Boral
and Pahari Sanyal

With Pandit Ravi Shankar

With Ustad Ali Akbar Khan

The young Anjani Bai Malpekar

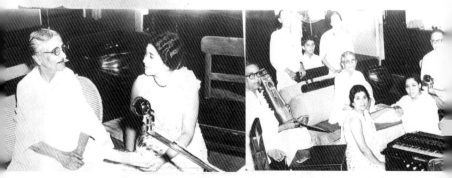

Recording Anjani Bai Malpekar, 1970s

With the Sabri
brothers of
Pakistan, after
a Raag Rang
mehfil

Lunch at home
to felicitate
Roshanara Begum

Jugalbandi with
Ustad Bismillah
Khan at Raag
Rang's silver
jubilee festival, Delhi,
1986; Vidya Rao on
the tanpura

Nainaji, as I remember her

Receiving an award from
the Ghalib Academy, Delhi

Receiving the Padma Shri

because the new world Mummy brought us to was so vivid and exciting—so different from anything we'd ever known before? The jingle of ghunghroos, the crisp tabla bols, the voices of those great singers… Or was it that I couldn't bear to let Mummy down by expressing even in my most hidden feelings, a sense of being deprived?' She then tells me how, meeting an old college friend, she remembered how she had felt: 'I suddenly remembered how I used to look at all her beautiful clothes—how many she had and I had nothing! I had thought then: "I must never let Mummy know that I feel this way."'

These clothes become, for Billy didi, the symbol of a lost way of life.

'You can't imagine what Mummy's wardrobe had been like before we moved to Delhi. She had the most exquisite sarees, rows and rows of shoes. Daddy would buy her beautiful jewellery to match each of her sarees. And she was always so exquisitely dressed. When Daddy died, she gave everything away. I think she couldn't bear to keep anything that reminded her so much of him. Only once she said to June and me, regretting that action a little—'I didn't think then that one day you two would grow up, that you too would want to wear beautiful clothes and jewellery.'

As the administrative director of Shriram Bharatiya Kala Kendra, Nainaji was indefatigable. There was the determination to preserve and foster cultural traditions on the one hand. On the other, she was eager to experiment. The many dance-dramas and composite programmes that she organized bear testimony to this. She worked on themes that explored music, dance and traditions of painting. One creation was the ragamala theme.

Taking several ragamala miniatures (paintings depicting the genius of a raga) she strung them together to form a visual narrative. The paintings' dohas (descriptive verses) and other appropriate verses provided a textual narrative. This text was set to music using the ragas depicted in the paintings, and then choreographed. It was a great success.

Around this time, a little before the move to Delhi, Nainaji returned to music as a singer, not just as an administrator, patron or listener. She had said, 'It was my friend Sharda Rao who encouraged me to do this. Sensing the emptiness in my life, Sharda had said, "You'll die if you don't sing. You have such a good voice. You must take up singing again."

'It was not an easy thing to do. The fact that I had not sung for seventeen years was problem enough. And then, there was the stigma attached to women who sang professionally. But I had been through so much that I had reached a point where I didn't care about anything any more. After all, what had I to lose? Respectability? Family honour? The good opinion of other people? None of these seemed important to me. One day, I travelled from Rajanagar to Delhi, I changed my name to Naina Devi and appeared for an audition at All India Radio.

'In those days All India Radio had a rule that no woman would be allowed to sing over the radio unless she could produce a marriage certificate or somehow prove that she was legally and respectably married.' Nainaji would often recall and quote the words of B.V. Keskar, the Minister for Information and Broadcasting, 'no one whose private life was a public scandal would be patronized.'

'Music was being rescued from the naach girls. Yet, because few women, except the naach girls were trained singers, to be a singer automatically meant an association with the ambivalently viewed world of naach, mujra and the kotha. I changed my name to Naina Devi so that no one would be able to identify me as a daughter-in-law of Kapurthala.'

But there was another reason for her new name—if respectable women did not sing, it was equally believed that respectable women could not sing.

'If I had sung under the name of Nilina Ripjit Singh, no one would have taken me seriously. I would have been considered an amateur, atayi, someone singing shaukiya, for her own amusement. But no one could have identified 'Naina Devi' as a non-professional. I began to sing ghazals and dadras. And then, I even sang English songs under the name of Ninotchka!'

Her eyes twinkle, and to my astonishment and delight, she begins to sing '*La vie en rose*' and '*Smoke gets in your eyes!*'. Then in 1964, she sang at her first major concert in Calcutta. The other artistes singing that evening were stalwarts like Nirmala Devi and Begum Akhtar. The concert was well received. From that point, there was no looking back. Naina Devi could now be identified with Nilina Singh. She was, unequivocally and by any other name, a singer.

5

Coming Home

As a singer she found herself again.
'I was reborn,' she says. She was 'born' this time into the family of musicians. Having moved away from one family at marriage, as, traditionally, all women do, then having lost this family when she was widowed, she now moved into her 'own' family, finding a home in the gharana of Rampur and the ang of Banarasi thumri, finding fathers and mothers in her many gurus.

For most women in patriarchal societies, life is a series of discontinuities, shifts, adjustments. From the moment she is born to the moment she dies, there is no place to which a woman belongs. She belongs nowhere and nothing belongs to her. She inherits nothing, receiving, at best, only gifts. She may be loved and acknowledged as daughter, sister, mother, but she herself is absent from the pages of history. She is the eternal outsider, the eternal exile, lamenting in the words of Amir Khusrau's bidai song:

> *Bhaiya ko deeni mahal suhani, hamka deeni pardes.*
> *Are sun Babul more kahe ko byahi bides.*

> To my brother you give your beautiful palace, to me, an alien land.

> My father, why did you give me away in marriage,
> to a life of exile?

The woman artiste shares this sense of exile and of discontinuity with all women. Like other women, she is acknowledged but not inscribed in the history of musical traditions. But learning, teaching and performing music provide her a space where she can experience and express a self separate from the given familial roles. A woman singer, especially one not born into a family of traditional performers, must, however, renounce the home of her birth, her religion, her relationships and all the excess baggage of appropriate feminine behaviour before she can claim this space as her own. It is a choice she makes and with it she sounds the first swara of the raga she will now sing all her life. She finds her home.

But where is that home?

I remember a rainy afternoon in Sawan. As the rain pours down and thunder rumbles around the house, Nainaji teaches me a Pilu thumri, a young girl's lament at being torn away from the home of her childhood:

> *Sainyaan barkha mein lene aye*
> *Babul se kehti, jhoola darati*
> *Eri ab jhoola jhoolane na paye.*

> In the season of rains my lord comes to take me away.
> But for this, I'd have asked my father to make me a swing.
> Alas! my friend, no swings for me now!

Almost without pause, Nainaji follows this with a kajri, a beautiful form typically sung during the monsoon:

Tarsal jiyara hamar naihar ma
Baba hath keena gavanwa na deena
Beeti gaila barkha bahar naihar ma.

My heart knows no peace in my father's house.
My father's stubborn—won't send me home
The season of rains passes, and I languish in my
father's house.

I hear the young girl in the song again, this time chafing
at being kept back in her father's house, yearning for her true
home with her husband. I hear her restlessness in her naihar;
I hear her unhappy, alone in her peehar. And I wonder where
her home is. Where is mine?

Is it just happenstance that Nainaji chooses to teach
me these two bandishes one after another? Singing them,
I realize that for me, perhaps for all women, there is no
place that we can truly call home. A temporary guest in the
homes of our birth, never quite assimilated in the houses
of our in-laws—where do we belong? In that moment, I
realize that we belong to nothing and no one but ourselves.
And because we belong nowhere, all places are home to us.
Home is where my feet are. What is here, now, is my home,
my life. I feel an extraordinary sense of release, a surge
of happiness.

And then I remember another thumri that she has taught
me:

Is bagiya mein more sainyaan milenge
Jora jori garwa lagaoon.

It is here, in the world-garden that I'll find my true
love,
And playfully, teasingly, I'll hold him close.

In Nainaji's life, while both families of birth and marriage were lost to her naturally and inevitably, she chose to renounce these familial identities, moving instead into other families—the family of music, the gharana, and the spiritual family of the pir.

≈》《≈

'I met with a lot of criticism. You know how unkind people can be…. As a singer my life was now very different from that of an ordinary housewife but I couldn't have cared less. I had left behind me all those notions of family honour, izzat, genteel behaviour. I had been through so much already. Nothing could touch me now.

'I used to sing over the radio. Ustad Ghulam Sabir Khan of Ambala, one of the finest sarangi artistes, used to accompany me very often. He grew very fond of me. He used to encourage me, teach me old bandishes, help me explore jagah in the bandishes that I already knew. He was my first teacher in those years when I returned to music.'

The 'jagah' that Ustad Ghulam Sabir was helping her find resonate for me in two ways. Khan Saheb was helping her find and explore musical 'jagah' within the bandish—spaces from where improvisations become possible, and the paths of those exciting, hitherto untraversed improvisatory 'rastas' within the raga. Equally, Khan Saheb's teaching must have helped Nainaji find spaces in her own life to rediscover herself and re-imagine the path her life would now take.

Sure enough, her life now took her down unexpected paths. This was also the time that she began working at the Shriram Bharatiya Kala Kendra. She describes her life there as the newly appointed director of that institution. 'The atmosphere was very different then from what it is now in

institutions for the performing arts. I used to live on Pusa
Road and many of the faculty also lived nearby. Ustad Hafiz
Ali Khan, the legendary sarod artiste and father of Ustad
Amjad Ali Khan, lived in the flat above mine. Shambhu
Maharaj lived a short distance away in Karol Bagh.'

There are many stories she tells me about Shambhu Maharaj.
No dancer was the equal, she believed, of this legendary
artist. But her favourite story was about the time when
Shambhu Maharaj met the queen of abhinaya, Balasaraswati.
She tells me about the meeting, about Balasaraswati singing
and doing abhinaya to the thumri 'Kaun gali gayo Shyam'.
Then it was Shambhu Maharaj's turn:

'Shambhu Maharaj pushed the harmonium in my
direction and began to sing. I followed him obediently, but
with a sinking heart, for he had begun to sing and do bhav
to this somewhat risqué dadra:

> Atariya pe chadh gayi ho gayi badnaam
> Paanch rupaiya sipaiya ke daibe,
> Das maange kotwal....

> Climbing up, sitting here in my pavilion
> I've lost my good name, my honour.
> I give the soldier five rupees
> The Kotwal asks for ten.

'What would Balasaraswati and the other listeners think
of these bawdy verses? Yet, as he sang and danced, I realized
afresh the greatness of this man. He depicted the nayika
climbing the atariya in a hundred different ways, depicting
our journey through life. The 'paanch rupaiya' and 'das
rupaiya' he interpreted as the five senses and the ten sense
organs that held us enslaved through this journey, and the
'badnaami' became the stain of our all-too-human failings.

'Balasaraswati's eyes filled with tears, and she cried out: "You are not just abhinaya samrat, you are also a great philosopher!"'

Nainaji laughs as she recalls how Shambhu Maharaj-ji would suddenly remember an old bandish: 'He would often come knocking on my door at five in the morning, saying excitedly when I let him in, "Rani, I've remembered that antara. Listen, this is how it goes!"' And then wistfully she adds, 'That kind of rapport and affection—you don't find it now.'

It was at this time that she began learning from Ustad Mushtaq Hussain Khan, who would be her guru till the end of his days. Khan Saheb was teaching vocal music at the Kendra. I began learning from him,' she tells me. It was as simple as that. For Nainaji, it was a homecoming. She was learning music again. Khan Saheb was 'like a father' to her. Writing about Mushtaq Hussain Khan, she refers to him as 'one of the most distinguished names in the annals of Indian music'. Prodigiously gifted, Khan Saheb, even as a child, showed extraordinary dedication. As a little boy, he would persist with his riyaz while all the other children whiled away their time in partridge fights or kite flying. His dedication helped him find acceptance as a disciple under such great musicians as Haider Khan, Puttan Khan, Mehboob Khan and Enayat Khan. Nainaji tells me how Khan Saheb's desire for perfection was so great that he gave up even sleep and food to dedicate all his time to riyaz. And at the young age of thirty-five, he became one of the court musicians of Rampur and soon the chief court musician. Playing one of the many recordings of Khan Saheb's singing from her collection, Nainaji draws my attention to his command over the raga that allowed him to sing it with equal ease in a brief three

minutes or elaborate it over an hour or more. She marvels
at his technique of voice production, modulation of tone
and his incredible range. She tells me that for her, his gayaki
represents the best and the finest in music.

She had met Khan Saheb before this, but they had lived
in different worlds. He was the great Ustad, doyen of the
Rampur-Sahaswan style of singing, and she, the young rani
of Kapurthala.

'I began learning from Khan Saheb in 1957. Khan Saheb
trained me in khayal gayaki, but I decided to specialize in
and perform only thumri, dadra and ghazal as I had been
singing these styles over the radio. I realized too, that these
were styles that suited my voice and temperament. My
early training with Girija Babu had also given me a good
understanding of the nuances of thumri gayaki. And, during
the years that I was married, thumri and ghazal were the
styles I had been able to hear.

'The riyaz of khayal was essential because thumri gayaki
bases itself on the foundation of khayal's understanding of
laya, swara, raga and tala. Contrary to what people believe,
no one can sing thumri without first having received taleem
in these aspects and internalized them. Khan Saheb taught
me khayal gayaki but he also taught me many thumris—
some of them his own compositions.'

Many years later, coming into close contact with Rasoolan
Bai, Nainaji absorbed many facets of her style too.

Nainaji spoke often of the purity of Rasoolan Bai's voice,
of the clarity of her swara articulation, the crispness of her
tappa, and the depth of emotion that she was able to convey
through a single swara or bol. She tells me how Rasoolan
Bai lost her home and all her belongings in a riot. Nainaji
came to her rescue, helping her ask for and receive some

medical and financial assistance, placing her case before the government, even writing to the prime minister. 'It's people like these who are a nation's greatest wealth,' she would say. 'It is our responsibility to care for them at all times. Rasoolan Bai was no ordinary singer. She could trace her musical pedigree back to Mian Shori himself, hence her command over tappa.' Indeed, Nainaji believed Rasoolan Bai's style was the perfection of thumri—one where swara, laya and bhav came together in a beautiful triveni sangam.

One of the most charming stories she tells is about Rasoolan Bai singing a chaiti. As she teaches me that same chaiti, she explains how chaiti is perhaps the most sensuous and erotic of all the forms included in the thumri genre. It portrays, she tells me, the rati-tripta nayika who herself signifies the season of early summer with its feeling of languor in the air and its atmosphere of contentment and leisure. The nayika is tranquil as she recollects and relives the love-play of the night before. At the same time this very erotic mood of the chaiti is equally and simultaneously understood as deeply philosophical. She explains the mood of this particular chaiti that portrays a young bride searching for a pearl lost from her nose ring—an erotic image that is equally the voice of the self mourning its loss of innocence:

> *Ihi thaiyya motiya heraya gaila Rama!*
> *Kahanwa main dhoondhu?*
>
> I lost it here, the pearl from my nose ring
> Where shall I look for it?

Nainaji tells me how Rasoolan Bai would sing it with so much expression and poignancy—now shy, now anxious, now teasing and saucy, now sorrowful, now seeking redemption—

that Nainaji, listening, would forget her mentor's old and wrinkled face, as it transformed before her eyes, into that of the young girl of the chaiti.

As she speaks, I realize that Nainaji's journey of learning, because it is thumri, because it is the journey of a woman not born into a musician's family and because it happened at a particular time, seems to reverse the ways in which we have come to understand the growth towards maturity. We tend to understand this process of growth—socialization, individuation, taking one's rightful and autonomous place in the life of the community—as a movement from the world of the mother, from the world of affection and emotion and the home, to the world of the father, reason and rationality, logos, the wider world. I wonder then if this journey to selfhood of a woman like Nainaji does not overturn all our accepted notions. For in a life like this, the movement has been reversed. One learns first from men, male gurus and ustads, who introduce the young aspirant to the discipline and the structured form of khayal or in an earlier time, dhrupad gayaki. Mastering that, the aspirant then goes mostly to women teachers, specializing in this emotional, fluid, apparently 'unstructured' form, where one has to go beyond rules, beyond raga and tala, to the realm of the purely lyrical, to pure emotion and communication. The singer learns to dissolve the boundaries that separate singing from dancing, poetry, theatre, speech. I wonder then if learning music, learning thumri especially, does not encourage one to question everything—ideas about the accepted ways of growing to maturity, about gender, about musical form.

One day Nainaji teaches me a deceptively simple dadra 'Kankar mohe laag jaihe na re'. It is one of the many dadras taught to her by Rasoolan Bai. 'How beautifully she used to sing this,' Nainaji tells me, as she explains to me the intricacies of dadra, its special jagah, its rhythm which must never be lost. 'Dadra should not be sung like thumri,' she warns. 'It is a completely different style. It has its own andaz.' Then to illustrate, she makes me listen to a recording of an old concert of hers. As I listen, Nainaji's thoughts go back to that morning in December 1974, to the ITC Sangeet Sammelan, when she had sung this dadra among many other favourites of Rasoolan Bai. It was a critical day, a critical concert. Halfway through it, Rasoolan Bai, now in Allahabad, had died. And in that moment, miles away, in far off Delhi, Nainaji, singing this purabia dadra had known without the shadow of doubt that she had died.

Rasoolan Bai had suffered a paralytic stroke. Nainaji had brought her to Delhi and nursed her through her illness, feeding her, giving her medicines, washing and cleaning her when she soiled herself, cheering her up through that bleak, terrible time. 'I am grateful to God that I had the opportunity to serve her,' she says now.

When Rasoolan Bai was better she decided to go to Allahabad. Before she left Delhi, she asked to be taken to Hazrat Nizamuddin's dargah. Prayers offered, the two women sat by the sacred tank whose water, legend has it, lit the lamps of the workers building the shrine when oil was denied to them. Rasoolan Bai gave Nainaji a simple silver ring. 'Wear this for me,' she said, slipping it on Nainaji's finger. Then she left Delhi and went away to Allahabad.

Some time later, Nainaji was to sing at the ITC Sangeet Sammelan. It was a morning programme—I see this in her choice of ragas, opening with a Bhairavi thumri and then a tappa in the same raga, followed by dadras and ghazals. 'I hadn't planned to sing these,' she tells me as we sit listening to this cassette recording. 'But on the way to the auditorium, I suddenly decided to sing the bandishes that I had learnt from Rasoolan Bai, and that she herself used to sing very often. I began singing. It was one of those good days when the very first note was so perfect, so true, that you knew this concert would go well. It was as I was singing '*Kankar mohe...*' that suddenly and inexplicably, the silver ring snapped and flew off my finger. My heart stood still for a moment. I was singing. I could not stop. An artiste never panics or stops in the middle of a performance. So I continued singing though I knew with a terrible certainty, as if it had happened before my eyes, that Rasoolan Bai was no more.'

She shows me a fragment of a silver ring, one half of the broken ring that she found after the concert, fallen in the folds of her saree, and which she preserved as a taveez, a talisman, a symbol of Rasoolan Bai's many gifts to her. 'I searched all over the stage for the other half of the ring, but I couldn't find it anywhere. It was incredible, but it seemed to have vanished into thin air.' Looking at the broken piece, she says, 'Rasoolan Bai sang all she had to, and she died. There won't ever be another singer like her. But even half of her andaz, half of her ring is gift enough.'

It seems to me that she is telling me something very important about what it is to be a shagird and a singer. She is telling me what anguish and joy there is in being one small link in the chain of affection and expertise that is a gharana. You know, you are so painfully aware, that you will never be what your guru is. You will never sing in quite the same way. But one half of that ring, part of that ang—and the word ang has a comfortingly material sound to it—has been given to you, is with you. The other half of the ring, the missing half, you have to provide. And that is what makes you a true shagird, but also a free and individualized voice.

I remember another dadra, handed down over generations through many voices to me: '*Sudh ai re balam pardesiya ki...*'

It is one of the first dadras that she teaches me. She tells me that she herself learnt it from Begum Akhtar who learnt it from Lachhu Maharaj. Lachhu Maharaj had, of course, also taught it to Birju Maharaj. Lachhu Maharaj had, in his time, learnt it from Kalka Prasad. Nainaji has heard that this dadra was a favourite of Kalka Prasad's, and that Bigan Bai, one of the finest singers of Lucknow used to sing it often. 'She was nothing to look at, but she sang this dadra so beautifully and with such feeling that listening to her, people's eyes would fill with tears.' Listening to her speak, I wonder from whom Bigan Bai learnt this.

I realize that this dadra that I have just received comes to me not in a clear, unbroken line, but in swirls and eddies. There is a direct line of musical descent through the male performers. Traditionally, among communities of male performers it is the men who learn and perform, not the women. Both blood and art are handed down from father to son. But running alongside this clear unbroken line of patrilineage and musical patrimony is the webbed pattern of female inheritance, the musical lines of the female performers, where blood and art are not necessarily congruent. Thus Kalka Prasad teaches Lachchu Maharaj and perhaps also Bigan Bai. Lachchu Maharaj teaches Birju Mahraj and also Begum Akhtar. But whom did Bigan Bai teach? Her name and her tradition are forgotten.

One reason, an important one, is that Bigan Bai never tied a ganda on the wrist of any of the people who learnt from her; though her own wrist might have spoken of her allegiance to one of the ustads or gurus from whom she learnt. What she learnt from her mother or from any other woman was not similarly inscribed.

Traditionally, women learnt from the ustads, and they also in turn, taught others. They were accepted as shishyas into a gharana. But they could only pass on knowledge, not the legitimacy of that knowledge, the legitimacy of lineage in a gharana—of blood or of music. Women could not perform the ganda-tying ritual for their shagirds, thus could not legitimize and 'introduce' their children or their shagirds to the world. So too, many stories are recounted that alert us to the fact that women often, received only part of the repertoire of the gharana. Much of this has changed now, and many women perform the ganda-bandhan ceremony for their shagirds. But Nainaji is uncompromising about this tradition. 'Women cannot tie a ganda,' she says.

I mourn that. I would like my wrist to carry the mark of her teaching. I would like to carry and show to the world an unbroken thread that links me to her, and through her to Rasoolan Bai, Girija Shankar Chakravarty, Moujuddin Khan, Begum Akhtar, Mushtaq Hussain Khan and a somewhat unknown singer called Bigan Bai. I mourn that she observes strictly this tradition where knowledge is the prerogative of the male line, and where women catch the fragments, anonymously, passing them on in turn, a significant part of the gharana, but never inscribed in its history.

But I see too, that she is right. The ganda is that unambiguous visible sign of gharana and musical legitimacy, of a genealogy that is at once based on patrilineal descent and the inheritance of secret knowledge. Traditionally, the link between women singers and their shagirds has been more blurred, less clearly defined. There are more strands in the web of this invisible ganda and they come from many, many places and voices. In an earlier time, when the only women performing were tawaifs, it appears they learnt from everyone, eclectically, almost indiscriminately. Ustads of vocal music, sarangi and tabla players, dancers and poets, mothers, aunts, and other women singers heard briefly at mehfils, even from the tastes and predilections of knowledgeable patrons. Equally by the early years of the twentieth century, it was the women singers who were the most sought-after by the new recording labels, thus introducing yet another strand of influence into their already complex gayaki.

I think of the bandishes Nainaji has taught me and I think of where she herself has learnt them. From Rasoolan Bai, Mushtaq Hussain Khan and Girija Babu, comes the bulk of her rich repertoire, the base of her ang and style. But there are so many other voices in this ang. The Bhairavi thumris, '*Shyam sundar se*' and '*Bhor bai rang daar*' come from the Dhrupad singer, Ustad Moinuddin Dagar. From Pandit Ram Chatur Malik she receives two of her best-loved bandishes—'*Piyari na pairab*' and '*Laagi bayariya*'. Pandit Shamta Prasad gifts her a treasure trove of kajris, purabias and dadras, such as '*Apne piya ko*'. She inherits from the dancers, Sundar Prasad of Jaipur and Shambhu Maharaj of Lucknow, horis and dadras eminently suited to dance: '*Khelat hori*' and '*Bajaaye jaa baansuri*'. Hafiz Ali Khan gifts her this Pilu thumri—'*Sainyaan barkha me lene aye*'. From Begum Akhtar, Siddheshwari Devi, Badi Moti Bai, Anwari Bai, innumerable thumris, dadras, kajris. From Anwar Hussain, the brother of the film star Nargis, dadras by the dozen; shers and ghazals from the poets Jigar Moradabadi, Faiz Ahmed Faiz, Qateel Shifai, Makhdoom Mohiuddin, Rifat

Sarosh. And from Benazir Bai and Isharat Bai and so many other now forgotten dancers and singers, dadras, ghazals and shers, learnt silently, stored away in some corner of her mind to surface years later when she returned to music. What she has garnered is a treasure rich in its diversity.

I realize then that any ganda Nainaji might tie on my wrist would be inadequate to express the patterns of her own musical inheritance and lineage. I realize too that what I lose in genealogical depth I gain in a kind of lateral spread and an absorption of many voices and styles that have gone into Nainaji's ang, which she so generously bequeaths to me. I look down now at my bare wrist and I seem to see there, a multicoloured ganda. It is there, real and reassuring, only not visible to mortal eyes.

6

The Secret of Love

In Nainaji's room hangs a large photograph of her pir, Aziz Mian 'Raaz Piya' of Bareilly. Among his murids, disciples on the spiritual path, I discover, are many musicians and dancers—Mushtaq Hussain Khan, Hafiz Ahmed Khan and the other singers of Rampur, Shambhu Maharaj and Birju Maharaj, Sabri Khan, Uma Sharma….

I ask her how she became a murid, and she tells me, 'It was through my ustad, Mushtaq Hussain Khan that I found my pir.' She continues: 'I had been learning for some time. My riyaz was progressing well.' Then inexplicably—but surely a motif in the life of singers—a sudden loss of voice. 'I had so much trouble with my voice, I just couldn't sing. I went from doctor to doctor but to no avail. Finally Khan Saheb said "Forget all these doctors! What can they do to help you? Go to the pir of Bareilly Shareef; he will cure you".'

'He took me to Bareilly himself. The first few times I tried to meet Pir Saheb, something would happen and I would not be able to go. Khan Saheb would comfort me saying "Jo mazaa intezaar me hai woh visaal me nahin" (the pleasures of the anticipation of meeting the beloved are far greater than the actual meeting). Eventually I did meet Pir Saheb. As soon as I saw him, he touched my throat and said, "From this moment, all your worries are mine. Go in peace; everything will be all right."

'I felt a sense of great peace, of relief, as if someone had lifted a huge load off my head. I knew with an extraordinary certainly, that nothing and no one could ever harm me. I was safe, and more than safe, alive in a way that I had not experienced before. When I left, Pir Saheb blessed me and said, "Ustad se lo taleem, mujhse taseer" (learn the techniques of music, its intricacies from your ustad, but the essence of music, its secret heart, take that from me) and he whispered a doha in my ear:

> Har ko har me dekh le murakh, Har dekhe hai tohe
> Dekh dikhaun, dekh rahi hai, ka dekhe hai mohe.

> Foolish one! See for yourself, there's truth in
> everything around you.
> Know yourself to be seen, watched over, judged
> every moment.
> Look to where I point—don't look at me! Look out
> to this Truth beyond words.

'I returned to Delhi. I was cured, singing again, and with his blessings, better than ever before. Truly, Pir Saheb had given me the elusive gift of taseer. This is not something that can be learnt or acquired through riyaz. It just has to be, to come spontaneously, like a blessing, like divine grace. It is through this gift of taseer that I have been able to do all that I have done—sing, compose, learn and teach.'

Every year since then Nainaji journeyed to the urs at Bareilly Shareef, and also the urs at Ajmer Shareef, the shrine of Khwaja Moinuddin Chishti, Khwaja Garib Nawaz.

This story prompts me to ask the question: what is taseer? How does a singer acquire it? Nainaji's story would suggest that taseer descends upon the singer like grace, a gift unasked for, a miraculous blessing.

But today, reading the wonderful introduction by Amlan Das Gupta and Urmila Bhirdikar to Alladiya Khan Saheb's autobiography, *My Life*, I discover other things. They point out that with mastery over the gayaki, it is 'the voice that becomes the site for anxiety, and this is not a simple question of musicality or sweetness.' Taseer, they point out is 'measured by the effect that the singer has on his or her audience...' It is the ability not just to delight, but to move deeply. With taseer, the power of the singer becomes 'an irresistible and constraining force' that can make the listeners weep or strike them with amazement.

Nainaji believed that she received from her pir the gift of this taseer. She would often say that thumri was nothing if it could not create asar, if it could not affect the listeners and move them very deeply. She would often say, very modestly, that this gift of taseer was all she really had: 'If people come to listen to me, if I have been able to achieve anything at all, it is thanks to this.'

I realize, too, that though Nainaji believes that all religious paths and all philosophies lead to the same truth, for her it is Raaz Piya who is her guide, and Sufism, her path. Her abiding interest in philosophy and her devotion to the path of Sufism is reflected in her love of a form like qawwali, considered by many to be of lesser musical value. Today, qawwali and 'Sufi music' are perhaps the most popular of all the genres. Yet, until quite recently this was not the case. Nainaji differed on this point and wrote at length about this form:

When Khwaja Muinuddin Chishti ... came to India and settled in Ajmer, he came in contact with Indian music

[which] occupied pride of place and played a vital part
in the social and religious life of the country. Devotional
music known as kirtan was heard in most ceremonies and
congregations. Influenced by this, the Sufis invented a most
fascinating blend of Arabic spiritual music known as sama,
and Hindustani music; this came to be known as qawwali,
qalbana, naqsh-e-gul, etc. The new syncretic music suited
Indian culture and the temperament of the people admirably
and attracted large gatherings to its mehfils. Qawwali became
the most successful method of preaching the tenets of Sufism
and the message of Islam.

Qawwali has played a vital role in the lives of the great
saints of the Chistia order. Singing and listening to qawwali
dissolves the ego, leading to the blissful state of wajd. The text
of the songs, which revolve around the concept of the lover
and the beloved, representing the yearning of the human
soul for the Universal soul are no doubt important, but the
vital forces that bring about the state of wajd are pulsating
rhythm and melody.

Nainaji tells me how Khwaja Qutbuddin Bakhtiar Kaki
stayed for a full four days in a state of wajd as he listened to
a Persian couplet sung by qawwals. She translates the verse:

> What is the secret of music? Why is it so
> enchanting?
> Music is the secret of love, and love, the secret of
> God.

'Sufism,' she tells me, 'is not so much a religion, nor even
a philosophy, as a way of life.' I realize it is for her, a way of
being, and moreover, inextricably linked with music.

Perhaps, because it is so important to her, she takes me
with her on this journey, to put my own feet on this path.

Perhaps, she believes that along with the musical heritage she bequeaths to me, this path is part of the treasure she wishes me to inherit. One of her kindest, most valued gifts has been her taking me with her to Bareilly to become a murid. For me, this event, this experience proves to be another step in a long journey of self-questioning and self-discovery.

One April morning I go to her home. I have returned the previous night from the dargah at Ajmer, and have brought tabarrukh for her from the shrine. I walk in to find Raaz Piya's grandson, Hasni Mian, the present incumbent of the gaddi, the sajjad-e-nashin at the Khanka-e-Niazi at Bareilly, sitting in her drawing room. It seems to me a strange and quite miraculous coincidence that I, just returning from Ajmer, should now meet the pir of Bareilly. It is, I will realize later, a momentous meeting. Pir Saheb asks me to sing, and without the accompaniment of any tanpura or anything else, I do sing.

A few weeks later, Nainaji tells me that there is a message from Pir Saheb summoning me to Bareilly to offer hazri at the shrine. I feel I am in the middle of a whirlwind of events. Something is happening and I am willing to let it happen, to go along with it.

Nainaji decides to take along the Kathak dancer, Nandini Singh. I know Nandini well. Often Nainaji has made me sing for Nandini to help us both understand the relationship between thumri and kathak better as she believes music and dance are different facets of the same art. She feels that a person cannot be a good dancer without a knowledge of music and vice versa. About thumri and kathak she says that theirs is a choli-daaman ka saath; two parts of the same costume. She believes that kathak, like thumri, has a deeper spiritual meaning. She has written:

This dance form depicts life. The three phases of life—Creation, Preservation and Destruction—are clearly reflected in the traditional order of its presentation beginning with thaat and ending with tatkaar…. The graceful gaits and pirouettes are symbolic of the cycle of life as well as of the Sufi concept of the whirling dance of the dervishes, Maulawi, which means 'whichever way you turn, you face God'.

Nandini Singh shares a very special relationship with Nainaji. Many years ago, her mother, ill and dying, had brought Nandini to Naina Devi. 'I'm going to die. I leave my daughter in your care. Make her an artiste, a kalakar.' For Nandini, therefore, Nainaji is a second mother.

Nainaji takes Nandini and me—two daughters—to place us both in the care of a spiritual father. She takes us to Bareilly to ground us in the spiritual lineage to which she belongs.

Bareilly is a blur of images. But I remember the entrance to the dargah, through a narrow lane, a small door. Entering, I find myself, magically in a space larger than the narrow entrance leads me to expect. I think then, the space within is always larger than the boundary that appears to contain it. We are, I realize, richer, deeper than we seem.

The dargah is festive in celebrations of the urs. There are people everywhere. They are either musicians, many of whom I recognize, or simple folk from the towns and the villages around Bareilly. Nainaji, Nandini and I are in a minority; it is primarily a male gathering. Nainaji takes us to Pir Saheb who ties a red thread, a ganda, on the wrist of my right hand and another on Nandini's wrist. He gives us gur and chana to eat, putting it into our mouths. My eyes fill with tears. Nainaji too seems overwhelmed. In spite of all the noise just outside, this room is silent and still. I can hear my blood as it runs through my veins.

Then it is time to give hazri, to offer our art at Pir Saheb's feet.

We move out into the aangan, the main courtyard. What was an empty courtyard when we came in, is now a darbar. A regal throne-like masnad, richly brocaded with flowers and birds, has been set up in the centre. Pir Saheb sits there, surrounded by his followers. Behind him I can see the tombs of his ancestors. One by one, the musicians offer their music to him. Then it is my turn. Nainaji has taught me a bandish, a dadra in Pilu, especially for this day. It is a composition of Mushtaq Hussain Khan Saheb's and one that he himself often offered at the dargah. So here is one more connection, one more link with the ancestries that I am discovering.

As I sing, I feel a strange sense of weightlesseness:

Laago mero dhyaan guiyan saanvare salone se

My friend, my mind is immersed in the beauty of
the dark one.

Before me is the pir, regal, kinglike on his masnad. He is spiritual preceptor, father, king, Kanhaiya. He is the living embodiment of all the pirs whose tombs I see in this aangan, the visible sign of the legendary saints Moinuddin Chishti and Nizamuddin Auliya; he is the dark one, the saanvara salona Shyam, the flute player. All these beings are held together for this moment, in Pir Saheb's frame, his presence. Whom am I addressing? And who am I, as I sing? I remember Nainaji's words: Whichever way you turn, you face God, and I realize afresh that this is so because all that is, all that one sees and hears and encounters is beautiful, divine, worthy of our deepest love.

The dadra I sing is a long journey into understanding the nature of my self, of my singing self, and of the world. It is a journey too, into understanding the meaning of lineage, its importance, and its complete lack of importance. I see the mint-new, bright-red ganda on my wrist. I remember Nainaji speaking of the inability of women artistes to perform the ganda-bandhan ceremony for their shagirds, and I remember my sadness at this. I think then, that perhaps this trip to Bareilly is Nainaji's way of acknowledging me as her own. It is her way of sharing with me her spiritual path, and at the same time, giving me a legitimacy in the mundane world.

This moment is one of quiet affirmation, of a sense of knowing who I am, of belonging, of homecoming. But it is also a moment that gives voice to questions that, increasingly, I will ask myself about the meaning of ancestry and lineage, and about the relationship between the ordinary, workaday world, and our spiritual paths. I know this ganda to be an umbilical cord that links me to the comfort and safety of the world-womb of music. But I know too that the womb is not our home. I remember the story of the sage Ramana Maharshi, who, discarding that other umbilical cord, the sacred thread, had wiped out history and genealogy, and empty of name, identity, or tradition, had travelled pathless, seeking the truth. I realize that to find my own voice, my own home, I will have to first cherish these ties that bind, and then, when the time comes, unknot them and travel on. I know that this pathless journey began long before this moment in Bareilly, and that it will continue long after this. I understand that moments like this are maqaam, resting places, oases—they are not manzil, the destination. And I know too, that perhaps there is no destination, that the idea of a destination is a mirage. I remember a line from a ghazal by Seemab Akbarabadi: '*Ye jalwagaah ke parde hain, jalwagaah nahin*', and I understand that this precious moment is but the parda that veils the miraculous beauty that I seek. I know then that this is an endless journey and that I shall walk this path all my life.

I am still walking that path, and it is one that both is and is not the path that Nainaji travelled. I don't know where it will take me. It is enough to know the peace of these maqaams, enough to be on that journey.

-»» ««-

Along with her deep interest in Sufi philosophy, Nainaji believed that the contribution of Muslim musicians to Indian classical musical traditions had been very great. She would often say that for the Muslim community of musicians, the commitment to a life of music was perhaps even greater than it was for any other community. She believed this was because they clung to it and served it despite the fact that among some sections of orthodox Muslims, music, because of its ability to delight and move the heart, because it also appeals to the senses, does not enjoy the status of a path to the Truth. In extreme cases it is even considered a hindrance to the religious path.

But Nainaji would cite the example of sozkhwani as demonstrating the commitment to a life of music. These forms are sung—or more appropriately—'recited' (soz padhte hain) during Muharram.

Singing, a somewhat suspect activity, was definitely banned during this period of mourning. But for singers, this would prevent the very act of worship itself, as, for them music is an essential part of their spiritual path. At a practical level, there was the question of how a musician was to go without work and therefore without earning during this period. And even more importantly, how could a musician do without his or her regular daily riyaz?

Hazrat Nizamuddin Auliya found a way out. Tanpuras and other instruments were replaced by human voices holding the shadja, the tonic, and the body itself became a vehicle for laya and tala with the rhythmic thud of breast-beating (maatam) that accompanies the recitation of noha. Sozkhwani was moreover considered to be recited (parhna), not sung, though its recitation involved every single technique of singing from meend to all the different kinds of taans. The texts recited were appropriately focused around the tragedy of Karbala and the martyrdom of Imam Hussain, the son of Hazrat Ali, and of his family. There could, therefore, be no objection to this 'recitation'. Then, while musicians were invited to recite soz at the houses of their patrons, they did not receive payment for these recitations—this was considered neither work not entertainment. Their survival, however, was ensured by the fact that they received gifts in kind—clothes, food and food grains.

So deeply did Nainaji believe in this tradition, that she would, every year during Muharram, organize a recitation of sozkhwani in her house. She even taught me a soz to recite at this time.

Something of this has remained and grown in my own life. I continue, every year to recite soz and noha at Muharram majlis, and also naat during the Milad organized for the Prophet's birthday.

In Nainaji's home, the sozkhwani that I heard was sung by male gharanedar musicians. This style of soz recitation draws on every technique and vocal modulation of classical singing. This is quite different from the soz that is recited by women in their majlis. The differences are both in the style of the recitation and in the texts that tend to be chosen. The women's repertoire is composed often in the style of folk music, rather than the complex style of the gharanedar ustads. Nor is there the use of the aakar that holds and anchors the recitation. And while the male repertoire tends to focus on the glory of the martyrs, their valour and their virtues, the women's repertoire tends to focus on the emotions of the women and on relationships. It is relationship, loss and pain more than valour and the glories of martyrdom that are the focus of this repertoire. Participating in the majlis, mourning the martyrs of Karbala, identifying deeply with the bereft women, I begin to understand the power of collective mourning—to articulate and release pains long held in the heart, to heal, to create a community that shares sorrow, but also hopefully moves beyond that sorrow in the act of witnessing, remembering and mourning together the tragedy of unnecessary, cruel and untimely death. The tragedy of Karbala is now not separable from the tragedies of Partition, Gujarat, Kashmir, the North-east, Vietnam, Iraq.... As I recite, I mourn with the women all these devastating tragedies, all these acts of unspeakable horror and cruelty. Music becomes a way for me to connect with the women around me, to share their pain, to ease my own, and to lament the pain of a cruel world.

Thinking again about what Nainaji has told me, it seems to me too that what she is saying is that you cannot be a true artiste without also somehow being a misfit, outside the framework of society and its institutions. As an artiste, you have to marginalize yourself. You cannot expect to be part of the established order and still be a true artiste. Perhaps it is this sense, this belief that ultimately the true voice of the artiste speaks from the margins, that leads to her concern for tawaifs. Perhaps her empathy for them has to do with the fact that during the long years of her silence, it was the music of the tawaifs alone that she was able to hear. She often tells of women she had met and spoken with; she marvels at their music, their ability to move the listener so deeply with just a brief phrase. 'They knew how to communicate, how to hold the attention of the audience. When they sang, it was as if they sang for you alone. They were extraordinary women,' she tells me. 'They kept a whole tradition alive; they were the repositories and transmitters of culture.' She tells me how they were trained in not just music and dance, but in poetry and philosophy as well, in the traditional sixty-four arts. And she tells me how, in an earlier time, the sons of noble houses were sent to the tawaifs to learn the art of conducting themselves in polite society—how to speak, how to behave.

She tells me sadly, 'That culture, those people are no more, and tawaifs are not respected as they once were.' She tells me stories of courageous, tragic women—how beautifully they sang and danced, of their dignity and poise, how gracious they were, and how brave. She tells me how deeply and loyally they could love, how much and how selflessly they gave—very often to men who exploited and then deserted them. She tells me about one such man, who believed that the bad luck that haunted him all his life was his punishment for having deeply hurt the tawaif who had loved him.

'They sang thumri the way they did because of their experience of life,' Nainaji tells me. 'Only someone who knows that love is doomed can sing that way, can bring to her singing the knowledge of such pain.' She tells me how hard she worked to help these traditional women singers find new forums for their art and to educate their children so they would grow up to have more options than their mothers had. Then she remembers something and laughing, tells me another story.

'There used to be an annual event—the All India Tawaif's Conference. One year, 1961, I was invited to it. But far from feeling angry about being mistaken for a tawaif, I felt proud. It meant that listening to me, no one could tell that I was not a traditional singer of thumri. For me this was a compliment; I was singing thumri as it ought to be sung.'

Then, looking at me, her eyes grave, she tells me: 'Never be ashamed that you sing a form that was once sung by these great women. Always bring to your singing the memory of those women and their pain. Be proud that you are heir to that extraordinary, though much misunderstood tradition.'

People often remember Nainaji not only as a singer, but also for the work she did for music and musicians. Nainaji believed that the cause of music was best served by helping those who made music, and so, much of her energy and time went into this task that she undertook, first personally, then through Raag Rang.

Raag Rang was founded by Naina Devi in 1961. Other founder members included royalty, musicologists and musicians: His Highness Maharaja Yadvinder Singh of Patiala, Ustad Bade Ghulam Ali Khan, Ustad Vilayat Khan, Pandit D.T. Joshi, Pandit Sunil Bose, D.P. Sen, Ved Prakash Gupta and Keshav Kothari. Raag Rang was a cultural organization with a difference. The name itself was significant—Naina Devi used to say that the words 'Raag', calligraphed to look like the Devanagri script, and 'Rang', calligraphed to look like the Urdu script, signified the fusion of Sanskritic and Islamic culture. For her this was the true spirit of Hindustani classical music. Raag Rang supported and fostered all music forms and dance traditions without preference for any gharana. Music was more important to Nainaji than the differences between gharanas; she saw all artistes as belonging to a single community. All manner of divisions were unimportant to her. And so Raag Rang organized programmes of music and dance of all styles, from all over the subcontinent.

'Music knows no barriers,' she would say, and she would go out of her way to organize a mehfil for an artiste visiting from Pakistan. Among the many therefore who sang at a Raag Rang mehfil were Roshanara Begum, Salamat Ali and Nazakat Ali, Amanat Ali and Fateh Ali, Mallika Pukhraj, the Sabri Brothers, Iqbal Bano, Farida Khanum and Reshma.

Remembering those occasions, she would break into the charming bandish sung so beautifully by Roshanara Begum:

> *Nimbua tale dola rakh de musafir, ayee sawan ki bahar.*
>
> Set my doli down under this neem tree; it's the season of the rains.

Raag Rang was perhaps the only cultural organization at the time to organize an annual festival known as the Naaz-o-Ada festival, that focused on the somewhat neglected forms of thumri, ghazal and kathak. Raag Rang sought not just to entertain, but also to inform and educate, as can be seen from festivals such as Bansuri, Rang Basanti and the Gharana Festival, which took up a theme and explored it both musically and intellectually. Nainaji also planned for Raag Rang to organize mehfils apart from the major festivals. She believed that the environment of the mehfil made it possible for the artiste to establish a rapport with the audience and that Indian music and dance were best performed and appreciated in the intimate atmosphere of the mehfil, rather than in the formality of a large auditorium. Through programmes organized by Raag Rang, Nainaji also attempted to bring about awareness not just about music, but about the 'underlying philosophy' informing various religious traditions. Writing about Ek Rang, a festival of music, that she conceived and planned, she said:

> Music is not merely a means of entertainment. Naad meaning 'sound' ... is the most powerful instrument for sublime communion with the Ultimate .... The Sikh gurus laid much emphasis on music and the classical ragas.... An entire system of classical music is derived from Sama Veda and the shastras; music is a part of the traditional form of worship in all temples. The haunting musical notes of the azaan herald the time for namaaz in the mosques while the Sufi dargahs throb with the fervent singing of qawwali.

Under Nainaji, Raag Rang became a symbol of musical fraternity. It was in her home, or as part of a Raag Rang festival or mehfil programme, that artistes from different gharanas came together in the spirit of friendship. And not just performing artistes. Writers, poets, scholars and actors—all contributed significantly to the growth of Raag Rang as an organization. Drawn by her presence, Raag Rang became a home for artistes of different genres and persuasions.

Nainaji's wish was that Raag Rang should serve the cause not only of art, but of artistes as well. To those who asked for it, she gave advice generously, telling young artistes of the Patiala tradition how Bade Ghulam Ali Khan used to sing a particular bandish, or describing to a young dancer, Shambhu Maharaj's andaz of bhav, working out colour schemes and costumes for one, helping another select the ragas and bandishes to be presented at an important concert. She tracked down forgotten singers and helped arrange for their voices and repertoires to be recorded. Innumerable artistes were looked after by her in their illness and old age. Many were cared for in her own house. Understanding the need for a room of one's own, she worked out a small housing scheme for artistes, an artiste's colony. She helped arrange scholarships for deserving young artistes and negotiated for financial support for the dependents of deceased masters.

As programme adviser at Doordarshan she recorded conversations between great artistes like Sundar Prasad and Shambhu Maharaj. Another, Tarikh-e-Thumri, was a conversation between 'the three reigning queens of thumri', Siddheshwari Devi, Rasoolan Bai and Badi Moti Bai. Each had her own special quality, her own special style, her individual perspective on the world. Nainaji recorded them conversing and singing, talking about their art, their lives and their dreams. As a result, this extraordinary programme provided a glimpse, not just of the beauty of a well-sung thumri, but also of the world in which thumri flourished.

On another occasion, she coaxed Anjani Bai Malpekar out of her self-imposed exile and persuaded her to talk about herself and her art, and to sing, so that 'the younger generation, who would otherwise never have had a chance to hear her, would get at least a glimpse of the art of this legendary singer.'

Nainaji tells me the story of this singer who was the disciple of Chhajju Khan and Nasir Khan of the Bhendi Bazaar gharana, and whose singing of Bhairavi was considered to be matchless. About her singing it is said that the perfection of her swara was unparalleled. The beauty of her singing was matched only by the beauty of her face and her soul. Inexplicably, at the height of her career, Anjani Bai decided to stop performing in public. Quite possibly this was in response to a meeting with Gandhiji. Anjani Bai, and Husna Bai of Banaras were among the women singers who met Gandhiji and expressed their desire to contribute to the freedom movement. Husna Bai composed and sang patriotric songs. Anjani Bai, however, took the decision to abandon what people viewed as a 'negative' profession and dedicate herself to a life of service to others and teaching her art to serious students. Nainaji convinced her to break her silence, just once, to allow herself to be recorded.

Telling me about this, Nainaji shows me a precious photograph. I see a beautiful woman standing by a table, her hand resting on it, the whole picture composed very much in the style of the photographic conventions of the early years of the twentieth century. The woman is Anjani Bai Malpekar, Mai as she was known. Like all others who knew her, Nainaji loved Mai for her beautiful spirit, her gentleness and generosity and admired her for her extraordinary musical gifts. 'She was so beautiful,' Nainaji tells me, 'that Raja Ravi Varma wanted to paint her, but she refused to pose for him. However, undeterred, and determined to capture her beauty on canvas, Ravi Varma would be in the audience every time she sang; he would return home and try to capture her image from memory.'

Nainaji turns the photograph around to show me what

Mai has inscribed on the back—'To my dearest Naina, who lives in my heart, whose image resides in my eyes....' She shows me a letter from Mai, a letter full of love and concern for her beloved Naina, and introducing its bearer, 'a young singer of our gharana, Suhasini Koratkar'. She shows me other photographs of Mai, now old, grey-haired and bespectacled, but still full of grace and beauty. Mai sits with Nainaji, speaking and singing into a microphone, and I sit with Nainaji looking at a photograph and listening to a taped recording of that historic moment. I listen as Mai explains the intricacies of Bhairavi and sings the lovely bandish *'Nindiya ayee re'* in that raga.

In the many stories Nainaji tells me, I see how she has helped so many people and preserved so many different cultural traditions and forms. I see too how deeply grateful people are to her. And repeatedly I hear from her and about her the word 'dua', the blessings and good wishes of saints, teachers, students, people she has helped. I see that dua is a recurring motif in her life.

It is a winter morning in 1988. I am at the dargah of Hazrat Nizamuddin Auliya offering a chadar in thanksgiving for her recovery from a stroke. It has been a terrible month, through which Nainaji has been in hospital, pierced in a hundred places by tubes and needles, her limbs connected to instruments that are ticking, recording, measuring her breath, the beats of her heart, the impulses in her brain. Now she is well, and miraculously, singing again. I remember the day when I had walked into her hospital room to find her sitting up in bed, her harmonium beside her, her fingers faltering a little as they ran over the keys. I had found and brought her a print of an eighteenth century Dakhani miniature painting depicting the silsila, the lineage of the Sufi saints of the Chistia order. In the picture, they are all there—Baba Farid, Moinuddin Chishti, Qutbuddin Bakhtiar Kaki, Nizamuddin Aulia and Nasiruddin Chiragh Dilli, with joyous disregard for geography and chronology. Each holds a tasbih, a rosary, while Khwaja Moinuddin Chishti is dancing in ecstatic haal. When I gave the print to her, she said that it was their dua that had made her well. I remember this as I hand over incense, flowers and a green, gota-edged chadar to the khadim at the dargah. He says to me, 'There was no doubt she would recover. She has the dua of the many people she has helped. She has the blessings of Mehboob-e-Ilahi, Hazrat Nizamuddin himself.'

Dua. What is it, I wonder. How does it work? How am I to understand it? How receive and give it?

Musicians like Nainaji believe that 'it is impossible to achieve anything in the world, or in one's journey of self-understanding, without dua'—of god, guru, mentor, peers and even juniors. Nainaji often tells me that all that she has achieved has been by the grace of dua. Equally, many believe that it is her dua that has helped them.

One day, Abdul Aziz, a young singer of the Patiala gharana says to me after he has performed at her house at the annual Raag Rang Raseeli Holi festival, 'I've heard that those who sing in Nainaji's house surely find success.' This is something I have heard from many others, that Nainaji's blessings, her encouragement, are a talisman for aspiring artistes. She believes this too. Once she told me, 'There is certain configuration in my horoscope that indicates that those whom I bless, achieve their goal in life.' This magic of giving dua is her ability to draw out the best in the people who come

to her, helping them to find their own centre, encouraging
them to stay with that truth, to speak from that secret place.
This is something that, in her words, 'sikhayi nahi, seekhi jati
hai'—you have to understand this for yourself. No one can
teach it to you, only perhaps point the way.

7

Raag, Anuraag, Bairaag

Almost to the end of her life, Nainaji was busy helping Doordarshan, AIR, the Sangeet Natak Akademi to record for their archives, the voices and styles of old, forgotten singers. It is no wonder then that she received so much respect and affection from her fellow artistes.

In 1965, Nainaji was offered a five-year contract as staff artist at All India Radio. She began her formal association with All India Radio on 26 November that year; soon after this she became director of programmes.

As director of programmes at All India Radio and then as programme advisor at Doordarshan, she worked with unflagging energy, translating her ideas into concrete programmes. There was, for instance, the television programme on the history of music depicting the courts of Akbar, Muhammad Shah Rangile and Wajid Ali Shah with music and dance performances by well-known artistes. Another was a series on the great masters of Indian music and dance. Yet another explored the ways in which different dance traditions would treat the same composition, while another presented different gharanas rendering the same raga.

There were many occasions when she got together with other singers to organize programmes that tried to recreate the spirit of old Banaras. One such mehfil was held on the banks of the Jamuna—a picnic-like all-night affair to celebrate Gulabi Chaiti. Remembering, Nainaji says, 'They were all there, Siddheshwari Devi, Rasoolan Bai, Begum Akhtar, Girija Devi, Bade Ghulam Ali Khan, the Dagars, Ram Chatur Malik.' This fact is more important than it might appear at first sight. Perhaps it is the scramble and competition for patronage, perhaps the struggle for survival in a world which increasingly espouses consumerism, but many artistes express that it is rare to find a place today where so many musicians can come together freely, simply to celebrate and share their art, 'Where else could this happen but in Nainaji's house through her mediation,' say many old artistes remembering these mehfils.

'At the Chaiti festival the singing went on all night. Sometimes one person would sing, then another. And then as dawn broke, we all sang, dangal-style, the chaiti "*Sej chadhat dar laage*".' Nainaji tells me what dangal means in music: she has often told me about the musical 'wrestling bouts' (for that is the literal meaning of dangal) that would take place at her home. One artiste would begin singing a thumri, perhaps '*Papiha pi ki boli na bol*', and each artiste would extend this with his or her improvisation. 'We would improvise— sometimes for hours—with a single line,' something that was fun but also 'a way by which we learnt from each other.' These musical conversations between artistes are a kind of mirroring that make possible the creation of new ideas. It is through this mirroring that takes place between singers, between singer and listener, between guru and shishya that musical dialogue deepens and flowers—'bol bante hain.'

Some of the stories she tells are side-splittingly funny. But behind the laughter, other emotions are evident—some stories are tinged with sadness, some are almost frightening. There was a time when she had begun learning from Ghulam Sabir Khan of Ambala. 'I don't know why,' she says 'but Ghulam Sabir Khan was very fond of me. Perhaps he wanted to encourage me and help me. He would show me how to elaborate a bandish, how to spin out its bol. He was no ordinary accompanist but a maestro in his own right.' A fine sarangi artiste, perhaps second only to the legendary Ustad Bundu Khan, Nainaji considered his music not merely sangat, but the very source of her style. It must have been this fact that later led her to say, that in order to really understand thumri gayaki, it was imperative to have had some taleem, some guidance from a sarangi nawaz. Sometimes, when we sit listening to old recordings of hers, Nainaji draws my attention to Ghulam Sabir Khan's accompanying sarangi, pointing out how he both supported and echoed her singing, and simultaneously created spaces for further and unexpected musical dialogue.

A Punjabi from Ambala, Ghulam Sabir Khan was a big man, so big that his sarangi looked like a toy when he held it up to play. His music had all the fine detail, delicacy and nuance associated with thumri. His heart was as big as his frame, and he had a delightful sense of humour.

One day Ghulam Sabir had come to Nainaji's house to teach her and guide her practice. Midway though her riyaz, she sensed, more than heard, some confusion and excitement outside. And she realized that her father-in-law had decided to pay her a visit. She was still singing incognito. What was she to do? Quick as a flash, quicker than you might expect so large a man to move, Khan Saheb jumped out of the window,

sarangi and all, leaving Nainaji to receive her father-in-law
in a room which bore no signs of her riyaz.

The thought of Ghulam Sabir Khan jumping out of the
window has something of the slapstick about it. Yet as I hear
this story, I also hear Nainaji's determination to sing, her fear
of offending her family, her consideration for the family's sense
of dignity, and Khan Saheb's kind protectiveness in helping
her, at what must surely have been some inconvenience to
himself, to keep the peace in the family and yet fulfil her
dream of singing.

Another singer Nainaji loved and admired was Begum
Akhtar. 'Lovers of Urdu poetry should ever be grateful to
Begum Akhtar for popularizing and propagating Urdu
ghazal. Had it not been for ghazal singing, especially that
of Begum Akhtar, Urdu ghazal would have been confined
to a handful of intellectuals only....' She wrote this after her
beloved 'Bibi's' passing away, recalling the happy times spent
with her and acknowledging her debt to this great artiste,
perhaps one of the finest exponents of the subtle art of ghazal
singing. Though ghazal suffers today from the appellation of
'light classical' music, Nainaji believed that it is by no means
an easy form to sing. In one of the brochures brought out for
a Raag Rang festival, she wrote:

Ghazal... is appreciated by lovers of music and poetry alike.
The literal meaning of ghazal is a tête-à-tête between the
lover and the beloved....

The artistry of the musician lies in his ability to give each
couplet a true musical portrayal. It is the singer's version of
the poet's creation.... One must have a thorough knowledge
of music for spontaneous improvization coupled with a deep
understanding of human psychology.... A good musical

rendering of ghazal is a beautiful fusion of the depth of khayal, and the romanticism of thumri, and is difficult to render effectively....

Another artiste whom she often spoke about was Bade Ghulam Ali Khan. With him and his son, Munawwar Ali Khan, Nainaji shared a bond of friendship and respect. She admired Khan Saheb for the perfection of his voice, his taiyari, his dedication, and his simple, innocent nature. She would often remark on the magnanimity of this man who, in a recorded interview at the Sangeet Natak Akademi, stated that the only ang of thumri gayaki was the Purab ang. The Punjab ang was, he claimed, the Purab thumri dressed in Punjabi ornaments. She would tell me about Bade Ghulam Ali Khan and his brother, Barkat Ali Khan, who '...with their keen aesthetic imagination enriched the style by successfully blending appropriate Punjabi folk melodies and Patiala-style harkats in the traditional thumris.'

Sometimes she would play for me a recording of Barkat Ali Khan singing the beautiful thumri '*Tum Radhe bano Shyam*' and marvel at his style, and technique, the richness of his voice. Or she would talk about Bade Ghulam Ali Khan and recall how Khan Saheb saw everything through the prism of music, how music was literally his whole life. She would remember how in his last days, bedridden after a stroke, Khan Saheb still insisted on singing, sitting up in the hospital ward, his sur-mandal on his lap.

The poet Jigar Moradabadi was one of Nainaji's close friends, and her repertoire included many of his ghazals. As she taught me this one, a favourite of hers, she said, 'For all their depth of philosophy, Jigar's ghazals are written in a language that is simple enough for anyone to understand.

And Jigar's verses are a delight to sing—they are intrinsically musical':

> *Duniya ke sitam yaad na apni hi wafa yaad*
> *Ab mujhko nahin kuchh bhi mohabbat ke siva yaad.*

> The cruelty of the world, my own loyal passion—all
> these are forgotten.
> All I know now is this extraordinary
> all-encompassing love.

Then she tells me another story. She tells me how at a performance one evening, she had sung this very ghazal. 'Jigar Saheb was in the audience and greatly appreciated my singing. The programme over, I went home and was fast asleep when there was a knock on the door. Imagine my surprise when I discovered the visitors to be none other than Jigar Saheb with some other friends.' The result: an impromptu mehfil at which not only Nainaji, but Jigar Saheb too, sang ghazal after ghazal till dawn.

Another day, she tells me a strange story—and the way she tells it haunts me for a long time:

'Once I was invited to a mehfil at a friend's house. A famous singer had been invited to sing and I was looking forward to hearing her because she was, musically, one of my idols. I admired her singing and looked up to her as a mentor.

'But what got into her? As she sat down to sing, in front of all these people, she suddenly began to insist that I should sing first. She wouldn't let me refuse. "Tumhe meri qasam," she kept insisting. I had only recently begun to sing in public and this was hardly the time or the place! I tried to reason with her—"How can I dare to sing when the audience is expecting to hear you?"—but to no avail. She would not give up her whimsical idea. So finally I did sing a little.'

She turns to me and after all these years, her eyes are still troubled: 'You know how it is—sometimes you begin well, your voice comes out perfect, clear and true, everything is just right, and you go straight to the hearts of your listeners. Well, that's what happened on that day. Then to my astonishment and horror, this great singer flew into a rage. She stormed out of the room and in the privacy of a small room that had been set aside for her, she burst into angry tears. She refused to sing. Bewildered, I followed her, but worse was to come. To my surprise, she turned on me. "You've insulted me," she said. "You did this deliberately to spoil my concert, to take away my listeners." I tried to plead with her. "That's not true," I tried to tell her. "I only sang because you insisted I should, out of obedience to you. Can I ever hope to sing even half as beautifully as you? Please come and sing. They're all waiting to hear you. It's you they want to hear."

'She wouldn't be comforted. Instead she turned away and said, "Why don't you leave me alone? Why don't you let me keep the one thing I do have—my music? You have everything—respectability, a family, wealth and social position. I have only my music and even this you want to snatch from me!" Somehow I calmed her down. Finally she sang, and beautifully, and all ended well.'

That incident led Nainaji to think about the mixed blessing that is the life of a woman singer. At that time few women from 'respectable' families sang professionally. For women who were from families of traditional professional performers, the ambivalence with which society viewed them must have been hard to bear. Thinking about that incident, which still seems to have the power to hurt her, Nainaji tells me: 'Because of the difficult lives they had to lead, many of the traditional performers were very complex personalities.' As I hear her speak, I understand that this complexity of nature is, in fact, not restricted to this one group of people. Perhaps we are all complex, perhaps we all suffer from insecurities, jealousy, anger; perhaps we all ache to be accepted and loved just for who we are, not for what we can do. I realize that by sharing this story with me, Nainaji has shown me that the path to full adulthood lies through a compassionate yet wise understanding of human frailty—the frailty of others, and ourselves.

There is a story behind every bandish she teaches me. The dadra in raga Pancham se Gara, '*Hamse na bolo*'—it was a favourite of Moujuddin Khan's and of Girija Babu's from whom she learnt it. It became one of the most popular pieces in her vast repertoire. 'People used to ask me to sing it at all mehfils and programmes.' She recalls one such occasion. 'It was in Calcutta. The mehfil had been organized at Marble Palace which had been decorated, complete with a Victoria, to create the ambience of Calcutta in the early twentieth century. I had finished singing and was about to get up when Pandit Ravi Shankar, who was sitting in the audience asked me to sing this dadra.' And Nainaji, teasing him good-naturedly, recalling the time when they were both young and he was a talented young dancer in his elder brother Uday Shankar's dance troupe said, 'I'll sing it, certainly, if you will dance to my song!'

She shows me a newspaper clipping, the *Telegraph*, dated 28 January 1984. There is a photograph in which Ravi Shankar has jumped up and hugged Naina Devi warmly. They are both laughing, and so is the audience, delighted at this affectionate joke.

These jokes, this affectionate teasing, this friendship between artistes—I will encounter them again and again in her life and in her stories.

It is 1986 and Raag Rang's silver jubilee is being commemorated with a four-day festival of music. I have only recently begun learning from Nainaji, so I am overcome with amazement when she insists that I should accompany her when she sings on this occasion. I voice my doubts but she brushes them aside: 'You can—you must.' She has planned to perform a jugalbandi with Ustad Bismillah Khan. In the green room of Kamani Auditorium, Nainaji and Khan Saheb decide what they will present half an hour later that evening. They choose the thumri '*Aangan ma mat so sundarwa*'. With its ambiguous poetry and its elusive musical structure, this thumri and its raga seem to epitomize the delicate ang of the Banaras style. In the green room, then later on stage, I watch them as they perform—conversing, teasing, asking and answering questions, mirroring each other.

This is not the first time Khan Saheb and she have performed together. There was a performance in Kabul in the 1960s, and both of them remember this event with warmth. Later, Nainaji will tell me of these jugalbandi performances with '...the shehnai wizard, the one and only Bismillah Khan, as experiences that I'll always treasure'. It has been, I realize, possible for them to work together so easily because it is the spirit of Banaras that they evoke each time through the genius of a thumri.

⋙ ⋘

Nainaji's home was a meeting place for all artistes. Hardly a day went by without a musician or dancer dropping in— from the legendary greats to unknown young aspirants. On other occasions, Nainaji would invite them for a mehfil followed by a meal, or a meal followed by an impromptu mehfil. It was on one of these occasions that I heard the great tabla maestro, Pandit Shamta Prasad sing, accompanying himself on Nainaji's harmonium. All afternoon, dadras and kajris rained down, one after the other, as he sang and I listened enthralled.

On another occasion, Nainaji opened her home to Ustad Vilayat Khan for him to rest and recover from a cataract operation, and I, walking into the house one day, had the astounding good fortune to hear him, not just singing, but teaching one of his shagirds, a beautiful bandish in raga Hindol.

'It's just like the good old days,' said Pandit A. Kanan, when he and Malabika Kanan were present at a small mehfil of Ustad Jafar Hussain Khan's qawwali that Nainaji had organized in her home. He must have been referring to the fact that not only was there this exquisite music, but also that the performance was taking place in the smaller, more personalized environment of a living room rather than a huge auditorium. Also, the listeners were themselves artistes—the Kanans, Kumar Mukherjee, Ustad Asad Ali Khan, Uma Sharma, Ustad Sabri Khan, Ustad Dayam Ali Khan and many others.

Listening to their conversation, hearing them break into an old bandish was an education in itself. The stories, jokes, discussions about music or about beloved singers now no more—sitting there, I would drink it all in and think how fortunate I was to be there.

Generous guru that she was, Nainaji's home was always filled with students. Many would come to enrich their repertoires. To name a few, Suhasini Koratkar, Shubha Mudgal, Madhumita Ray, Parul Banerjee, Roma Mukherjee, Uttara Dutt, among others, were her disciples. With each one she shared a special relationship.

One day she plays for me a recording of Professor Sunil Bose singing Binda Din Maharaj's composition, '*He Govind, He Gopal*'. This composition has many special memories for her. Now as we listen, she encourages me to see the jagah Sunil Bose is finding, the meanings and nuances he is coaxing out of this bandish. She tells me that in her childhood it used to be very popular in Calcutta. All the famous baijis knew it and sang it often. It was taught to her and to Sunil Bose by Girija Shankar Chakravarty. The poetry of this composition is inspired by Surdas's pada '*He Govind rakho sharan*'. Both deal with the theme of Gajendra moksha and it is, both in content and in spirit, more bhajan-like than the usual thumri. It is the style of singing that allows it to be included in the thumri repertoire rather than as part of kirtan or bhajan, just as the gayaki, the andaz of singing decides whether a piece of poetry known as ghazal is musically tarannum, ghazal or qawwali.

As she listens, Nainaji's eyes fill with tears, remembering Sunil-da's death. 'I was with him when he died, stroking his head, singing this bandish for him':

> *Thhake sab kar upaay ek aas teri*
> *Doobat hoon ab to Nath, karahu nahi deri.*

> Rescue me now, you who are my last hope.
> Lord, you see me sinking, don't delay.

'He died as I was singing—peaceful and happy.'
This bandish has other associations.
Picture a little child running down to the banks of the Ganga in Banaras. She sits by the ghat watching the sun rise on the eastern bank of the river; the grey water gently laps the stone steps. Before her, the child sees bajras, boats. In Chaitra, at the time of the Burhwa Mangal festival, these

will come alive, each boat transformed into a rang mahal, a mehfil space. The voices of the great singers of those times—Achchan Bai, Malka Jan, Rajeshwari, Vidyadhari—will waft over the water to the less fortunate crowds sitting on the ghat, eating jalebis, chewing paan, listening, as do the rajas and nawabs on the bajras. The child will hear these immortal voices singing the beautiful folksy styles of chaiti and ghato.

But now, in the cool dawn, the bajras are silent, sleeping. The child has set afloat a small leaf boat; a lamp set in a bed of marigold flowers. She watches as it bobs bravely downstream towards Manikarnika Ghat where smoke curls up ominously reminding her that death is but another face of this beautiful, throbbing, vibrant city. The sun is just rising. Night's darkness yields place to grey and then to soft pinks and yellows; the silhouettes of the ghats, boats, temples fill with colour and detail. The child hears the sounds of birds, temple bells, prayers. And then over these usual morning sounds, the voice of a woman singing. It is a beautiful voice, sweet and rich and full of feeling—that mixture of sadness and wisdom and love that can only be described by the word soz. Drawn to the music, the child traces her way to the alcove on the ghat, where a woman, dressed in white, is singing Binda Din's famous bandish, '*He Govind, he Gopal, suniyo Prabhu mori*'—Hear my plea, Govind!

She is there every day, singing the same song. She sings in the andaz of thumri, but the music is suffused with a numinosity that takes it beyond styles and gharanas. The child is there too, every day, listening and looking.

Then one day the woman is not there. But her voice and her eyes remain in the child's heart.

'I cannot describe such beauty,' she tells me now. 'It was the memory of that unknown woman's singing and her large beautiful eyes that guided me to choosing Naina Devi as my name when I began to sing over the radio.

'I tried to find out who she was, this unknown woman, with whom I had not exchanged a single word, yet who was and still is, so much a part of me. Much later I discovered—who knows if this is the truth—that she was once a famous tawaif who had given up everything—possessions, jewellery, lovers, fame. Donning the white saree of the renouncer or the widow, she sat by the Ganga, singing in the thumri mode, Binda Din's prayer for deliverance, waiting for that moment of death which is really the moment of visaal, union.'

I have heard this story before. It is the story of so many women, the story of Ambapali, of Sufan Moti, Madhavi and Manimekhalai. Stories of women who were courtesans, and then one day, gave up all their wealth and comfortable lives to become wanderers on the spiritual path. The silence of death, the stillness of renunciation are never far from the colour, the noise and bustle of the tawaif's life. Her other face is that of the bhikkhuni, the jogan, the sufan. So often have I heard this story that I realize it is a 'real' story, a story that exists in a specific time and space, but it is also a 'true' story, in the sense that it is an eternal, mythic motif. It is the archetypical narrative of the tawaif.

As I sit listening to Nainaji, these other stories come back to me. I wonder, as I have often done, if it is not the power of these stories, the coming together in them of the two seemingly opposed realms of the erotic and the ascetic, that speaks to the depths of my own being, and that has led me to thumri, to finding the meaning of my own life through an involvement with this lovely musical form.

Sitting in Nainaji's room I travel miles and centuries. I remember again the story of Ambapali, famed courtesan of

Vaishali who met the Buddha, heard him speak, then invited and received him as an honoured guest in her beautiful house. Then one day she cut off her beautiful hair, gave up her rich robes for a bhikkhuni's patched garment and entered the nunnery.

Why did Ambapali, famed courtesan, give up her life to become a bhikkhuni? Was it the great compassion she experienced? Was it that for the first time someone saw her as a person, as worthy of respect, not just as an object to please, to entertain, to enhance the prestige of another, to enrich the state? I wonder then if Ambapali and the woman on the ghat, circumscribed by the given circumstances of their lives did not choose, joyously and self-consciously, this path of renunciation.

In these stories then I hear these women to be saying that for them, as for me, as for us all, the path is but a metaphor for our choosing, our determination to journey, to search. I see that this story is my story too, as it is the story of every woman who is an artiste. Because while all artistes confront the paradox of the ascetic and the erotic, perhaps for women this is experienced in a particularly poignant way. For the woman singer, for the thumri singer, there is always the memory of the tawaif. The tawaif performs for an audience, revels in their admiration and applause, is thrilled by a responsive audience, speaks to each person, directly, completely without barriers, seduces each one, insists that each person, for the brief lifetime of the performance, fall irrevocably in love with her who is the nayika. Yet she sings for no one. Some singers say they sing for God, some to please their own exacting selves, but all are conscious that there is no external other in this love affair. There is a hint of this in the word 'shringar', which means both love and desire, but also to adorn. Shringar does not set up a hierarchy between the person or object that is adorned and the adornment. Adornment, embellishment, decoration—of the self or of the music—are intrinsic to the self and the music; they are its 'lakshan', the markers by which it is known.

The tawaif is aware that she is shringar personified. Her work is to hold up the mirror of desire to her audience, to confront the listeners with their own desire, their nature as desiring, desirable beings. She lives all her life pleasing others, seemingly unidimensional, living on the axis of 'kama'. Then one day she gives it all up, enters the monastery, sits singing by the Ganga, wears the green robes of the sufan.

There is a mirroring here of the world of the senses and of the ascetic's death-like stillness—of complete indulgence and complete withdrawal, of form and emptiness, of raas and samadhi, of anuraag and bairaag.

The tawaif's act of subversion is the wresting of power to be an agent, not merely an object of desire. She goes beyond this eternal cycle of dark and light, up and down, action and reaction—she transcends it by renunciation. Yet she renounces it without revulsion of what has been. This, I believe, is a joyous bairaag.

It seems to me that because we live in a time when rational linear thinking dictates the way we tell stories, these narratives are structured as a progressive development, as a movement from one point to another. But this is not the only way time unfolds. Time is not only linear. It is also cyclical, also pendulum-like, also timeless, still. The woman singing in the kotha is simultaneously the woman singing at the ghat. No time has elapsed between one face and the other. The noise and confusion, the sights and sounds of Banaras are not different from the stillness of Sarnath.

8

An Endless Raas

In the last years of her life, Nainaji seems to go back to her childhood, to its culture and environment. In those years, when I go to her house, the kitchen is redolent, not with the fragrance of nutmeg, clove and cardamom, but with panch-phoran and mustard oil, fish and coconut. She has always preferred rice to roti, but now Bengali spices and Bengali food is what she, and I with her, eat every day, unless there are guests invited over. Bengali food replaces the Lakhnavi cuisine that was once her staple diet.

When I arrive at her home in the morning I find her sitting in her room with her breakfast tray, still wearing her quilted dressing gown with its design of mauve flowers. Her face is still soft with sleep; she has not yet disentangled herself from dreams that she recounts to me of her childhood home in Calcutta, of her mother, of school friends, of Mejdi. She takes a special delight in speaking the language of her childhood, and of being with fellow Bengalis. Sometimes, unexpectedly, even her pronunciation changes, reflecting the long-forgotten accents of her childhood. And in keeping with this return to her beginnings, she often sings Bengali songs.

I remember this one, from the Shyama Sangeet repertoire. One of Nidhu Babu's compositions, it employs the typical tappa-style phrases—the unexpected and extraordinary mix of the styles of kirtan and tappa. The song is in praise of Kali:

> Shiva's matted locks,
> Ram's neatly coiled jooda,
> A peacock feather in Shyam's crown,
> But my Shyama's hair is wild and free.
> In Ram's hand, a bow and arrow,
> In Shiva's his trishul,
> Shyam holds his winsome flute,
> But in my Shyama's hands, a hideous skull.
> Ram, resplendent in a king's robes,
> Shyam, radiant in his pitambar,
> Shiva wears a tiger skin,
> But my Shyama is clothed in nakedness.

Nainaji teaches it to me, disregarding my struggle with the language, explaining some of the words that I do not understand. One night, a few weeks after her death, this day will come back to comfort me, as I dream inexplicably, of singing a thumri in praise of Kali, and dreaming, will understand and say to myself, this terrible image must be sung into being with tenderness and love. This skull, this bloody tongue, those staring eyes—these are her shringar, her adornment and beauty. And I will wake to remember again, this strange, precious gift from my guru that brings together the beginning and the end of her life, and that blurs and softens the dualities of my own.

But that day, as I sit with her, learning this song, she tells me how as a child, she had first heard it and learnt it in Banaras, from a beggar woman named Khendi.

Khendi was ragged, sickly and quite hideous. Her skin was rough and scaly, covered with sores. Her pock-marked face had caved in—she had no teeth and the bridge of her nose had been devoured by disease. Khendi claimed she had been a baiji once, and you could believe that when you heard her sing. She would come to Nainaji's grandmother's house to beg for food, clothes and money, and even the occasional cigarette.

'Just one cigarette!' she would whine, or else, smacking her lips, remembering perhaps sumptuous past meals, she would wheedle, 'Make me a mamlette (an omlette), a mamlette, please, for hungry Khendi!'

Nainaji tells me, 'I would sit talking to her as she ate. And sometimes, in response to my begging, she would sing this song for me. When she sang, she was not Khendi, the beggar woman. You forgot her strange, broken face, her rags and tatters. There was only her voice—just her sweet, powerful voice.'

As Nainaji speaks, I seem to hear Khendi. I hear a rich voice singing this bandish in Khamaj as if it has traversed the rastas of that lovely raga many times. Khendi sings as if she knows Khamaj, as if she knows the raga the way a mother knows the body of her baby. She travels Khamaj's landscape without map or compass, without accompanists or instruments, without fine clothes or jewellery, or listeners. Khamaj lives in Khendi's voice. Khendi sings in Nainaji's speaking. And as Khendi sings, as Nainaji's speaks, the great goddess stands before me—here, now, real—in all her terrible beauty.

Who was Khendi, I wonder, as I remember another story that, gentler in its contours, Nainaji tells more often—the story of another woman, also in Banaras, also singing, also once a baiji. But this woman is beautiful, dressed in clean, white clothes. Her face is whole and serene, and she sings of the compassionate Krishna. Khendi and that unnamed woman of the luminous eyes, and a little girl listening. Are they three people, or two, or one?

And I, a fourth, a listener twice over—singing and living again those songs, those lives—I understand again, with a burst of wondering joy, that beauty and ugliness are but mirror images of each other, as are passion and renunciation, birth and death. And that it is music, the flowing river of raga, that enables me—enables us all—to travel from one apparent extreme to the other and to know them to be one in essence.

-»» ««-

Nainaji and I are sitting out in her garden on a crisp winter morning. Sunlight streams through the leaves of the pipal tree under which she had discovered a simple grave that she believes is a pir's mazaar. I am snipping dead leaves and pulling out weeds from a bed of nasturtiums. She is still weak after a long illness and sits small and frail in her chair. The frailness is deceptive; I know how strong she is. I marvel at this strength that has pulled her through so many difficulties, and now, through a major illness. I am thinking of all that she has told me, all the stories she has shared with me.

She is thinking back, too. Her eyes are far away. She says, 'I've lived a full life. I have my children and my shagirds. I've visited the palaces of kings and nawabs and the huts of impoverished singers. I've been close friends with Nobel laureates and kings and unknown dancing girls. I've prayed in dargahs, in temples, churches, gurdwaras. I was born into a Brahmo family; I married into a Punjabi royal family. Some of my most cherished memories are of the ghats and temples of Banaras; my pir is a Sufi saint... I've seen so many

things in one life. I've danced for Anna Pavlova, I've lived
in near-parda, and I've sung for audiences all over India.
I've watched my beloved Mejdi die. I've known adulation
and fame. I've been insulted by orthodox people for singing.
And I've really enjoyed life—everything, the good times, the
sad times.'

She seems to be echoing the lines of Qateel Shifai's ghazal
that is one of her favourites:

> *Kat gai umr ab kis tarah Qateel*
> *Wo buri thi ki bhali, yaad nahi, yaad nahi.*
>
> I've come to the end of my life now, Qateel
> Was it bad? Was it good? I don't know.

'All the troubles I went through after my husband died—
indeed, his death too—these things had to be. It was because
of all this that the artiste in me was born. Imagine, if life had
been easy for me, if things had worked out "happily-ever-
after", I may never have been a singer!'

I understand. It is in the crucible of life's hardships that
we learn to find our true selves, our true love.

I wish I could end this story here. But life never gives us
neat endings. And Nainaji's story winds on after this day of
gentle acceptance.

On 26 February 1992, Nainaji was admitted into hospital
with a mild stroke. That day marks an important change in
her life and mine. She is no longer the person I knew. I try
and put myself in her place, but she seems to elude me. She is
in turn exhausted and vulnerable, upbeat and cheerful, angry
and defiant. The ease with which we once spoke—I can no
longer be sure of that. Then I realize that she is teaching me
one of the most important lessons of my life: she is teaching

me what it is to grow old, to be ill, what it is to be close
to death.

I see her moving away from all that she has known and
been, all endeavours, hopes, works. I see this when she
teaches me a ghazal:

> *Duniya me koi lutf kare ya jafa kare*
> *Jab mai nahi bala se meri kuchh hua kare*

> Now, neither love nor the pain of betrayal touches
> me.
> When I'm no more, what difference does it make.

In what she does not say, I understand that she is teaching
me about the transience of life, about the fleeting nature
of our greatest achievements and our deepest desires, that
few things are important in the end—that life and death, as
someone put it, are not serious alternatives. I understand,
as I live through these days with her, that one's life, one's
thoughts, one's self—all have their place, their meaning, and
at the moment that they happen they are real; and then they
are gone. I understand her to be teaching me that in the end
it is to death that we all belong. In death we are all equal.

I try and think about this in those days that now seem so
far away.

I find that suddenly something has changed. There was
a time when my guru was like a mother to me. She still
is—but the roles are also now somewhat reversed. It is for me
now to nurture, protect, humour her; my guru is respected
as before, but now also loved as a child.

I try to understand this new world she is encountering.
For if death comes to all people, if the presence of death is
a reality for each one of us, then surely, at least in theory,

I should be able to be with her in this time. And so, I try
and understand what death means to different people. I ask
myself: how do artistes experience death?

For the artiste the death of loved ones, especially of the
father, is a terrible event that leaves the young artiste not
only fatherless, but guruless. In Nainaji's life this assumes
another pattern, her guru is lost to her through the event of
marriage. The death of her husband, tragic and traumatic,
becomes the point for her to return to her guru and find
herself as an artiste again. And gurus and pirs provide her
with other families—the family of music, the gharana, or the
spiritual family of the pir and his murids. Her gurus are like
parents to her, and so is the pir a loving protecting father.
'Rasoolan Bai was like a mother to me,' she often says. Her
relationship with Mushtaq Hussain Khan's children is truly
one of affection shared by siblings. And once, at a time of
great distress, as she sat crying helplessly at the dargah in
Bareilly, Raaz Piya had said to her, 'Why do you cry? Am I
not here to help you? Am I not your father?' And of course
shagirds are her children. I could echo her own words and
say, 'She is my mother, as much as is the mother who gave
birth to me.'

But it is not only the death of loved ones that we must
learn to face. Understanding death is to come to terms with
one's own mortality; it is to confront the inevitability of one's
own death. There was a time when Nainaji used to say, 'I've
lived a full life. I can go now, happily.' She used to say, too,
recalling Rasoolan Bai's suffering: 'May god grant me a quick
end. May I live only as long as my body is able and my limbs
functioning. May God protect me from the ignominy of
dependence, from the terror of a slow lingering death.' Now
she rarely speaks thus. Is it a fear of death that prevents her

from speaking about it, a fear that the words might summon the event? Or is the refusal to speak born out of a complete acceptance of its inevitability? Is it an unwillingness to share her conflicting emotions with me, a younger woman, so much further away—but only theoretically so—from death's door? I know she is aware of her own life rushing to its end. I try to tell her that death is no respecter of protocol, age, our notions of correctness. I may go before she does. Death may choose to come late or early, painfully slow, or swift as lightning. Wilful child, manini nayika, ardent piya, death comes when it will. Not all our wooing of it, not all our frantic attempts to hide from it make the slightest difference.

I try to tell this to Nainaji, but I find I cannot. I know, as she must do too, that for me the event of death is still only an idea. Death's presence is in her body as it is not in mine. I understand that this is a journey she has to make alone, as I too will have to one day. And it is a journey she will make in her own way, defining courage as she will. I can only watch from a distance and wonder: should one 'go gentle' then or should one 'rage against the dying of the light'? Does acceptance spell courage, or does resistance? Or are these foolish questions that overlook the fact that in one's dying, as in one's living, a person displays a style, and perhaps it is a style that one has been crafting over the years, readying for this last great performance.

It seems to me that to be a singer, to have the craft and style of a singer is to have the possibility to understand and meet this moment of death. In a sense, all of life is a preparation for that inevitable moment. Across the journey of life are scattered smaller deaths—the passing of the seasons, the loss of youth and innocence, the imperceptible fading away of love. Because music exists only in time, because simultaneously it marks timelessness and shapes time, a singer is perhaps more easily able to confront and understand the truth about death. In many ways death is present in every moment of musical life. A swara dies, is lost forever even as it is born. The tala's sam is both its beginning and end. Bhairavi begins the morning and ends the night. The singer, sharply confronted every moment with the fact of death, is perhaps specially privileged to understand it. In music, there is space for the singer to look at death unafraid, to know this great unknowable, unspeakable mystery. But this is only a possibility. The singer has to actualize it, consciously, willingly.

I was still struggling with the understanding and acceptance of this when after a brief illness Nainaji passed away peacefully. She died on 1 November 1993, a day after the full moon of Sharad, as the year entered the auspicious month of Kartik.

As I see her small, still form, I hear her voice again: 'From Sharad poornima to Kartika poornima is the time of Krishna's raas. If you sing at this time, heaven is yours.'

I remember her words and think to myself, perhaps she chose this moment to let go of life. I think of her, singing eternally now in Brindavan, dancing an endless raas. I think of all the years I have spent with her. I think of the years that lie ahead, empty years, bereft of her voice and presence. Then I realize that I have to learn to let her go. I realize that the purpose of her life was her life, not my need of her. I knew her for a while. For a few years, our lives flowed together. Now she has gone, and so, in my way must I too move on. I cannot stop the tears, but I will not grieve. She would not have wanted it so.

-≫≫ ≪≪-

I remember a trip to Ajmer we had made together. It is early in the morning, but already past the hour of azaan. Below in the courtyard, a large family of pilgrims is cooking breakfast. They are from Gulbarga in Karnataka, and have travelled all this way to worship at the shrine of Khwaja Garib Nawaz. Why are they here? To fulfil a vow, to offer thanks, to pray for help at a time of dire distress? Or do they come simply because they need to be here, just as they need to eat and drink and sleep? They have a story, so do I, so does the woman still asleep in the room I have just left. It seems to me then as I watch the smoke of their cooking fires curling in the cool morning air and hear the children crying, quarrelling, playing, that every person's life is a story, only some live it more consciously and creatively than others. Our stories interact with the stories of other people, with the story of our times, with history. These stories shape each other. It is, I realize, at the intersection of personal narrative and historical event that a life is lived.

I think of all that Nainaji has told me and shared with me about her life and about music. I see how, in her telling, she has woven words and incidents to make her life meaningful. And I see how, I, listening to her words, make my own patterns and meanings. Her words give me the threads to weave my sense of her story, and indeed to weave my own story too.

I remember her telling me about Khwaja Qutbuddin Bakhtiar Kaki who breathed his last, listening in a state of wajd to a verse of Sheikh Ahmed Jam. Nainaji would quote the verse and explain it:

> *Kushtagaan-e-khanjar-e-tasleem raa*
> *Zamaan az gheb jaan-e-deegar ast.*

For the victims of the sword of divine love
There is, every moment, a new life.

And I remember that for her this 'divine love' was nothing
but the essence of music. Hers was a life totally absorbed in
music. Of course, there was an awareness of political and
other matters, and a recognition of the fact that these events
affected, even controlled, the life of music and her world. But
it seemed that to her these were not the real stuff of life. If
ever I asked her, for instance, about Partition, an important
moment in the lives of most people of her generation, a typical
reply would be: 'It didn't affect us much. We were in Shimla
then.' I wonder how it could not have and then would accept
what she said. I realized that for her, since music could not
be partitioned, lines drawn on a map were meaningless. She
would speak of the singers of undivided Punjab, or of the
mazaar of Baba Farid at Ganjshakar, and how she would like
to go there again, or how Fateh Singh of Pakistan couldn't go
to Ajmer Shareef because his visa did not cover a visit to that
town. And I would realize that for her Partition was more
a nuisance, involving passports and visas, a problematic
rupturing of the smooth flow of cultural traditions, that in
themselves were indivisible. Tappa comes from Multan, but
has 'settled' in Banaras. Banarsi hori thumri is equally the
child of hori dhamar of Brij, and the Kafi of Sindh. Partition
has meant for thumri singers on either side of the border, a
separation, a judai from one or the other of these parents.
Partition ruptured the ground of musical traditions, but the
traditions themselves survived.

In Nainaji's own life, the ruptures and breaks, the
discontinuities, came as they do for all people, from the
accidents of destiny and from the events of the life cycle that

disrupt the lives of all women. These acquire meaning in the context of her musical journey.

It seems to me that it is precisely these breaks and ruptures that characterize the lives of most women that helped Nainaji realize the self that she forged, even as she spoke with me. Marriage and the break with music was followed by widowhood, which could so easily have meant fading into the shadows. Instead, this crisis became the turning point; it was from this point that she began to rethink her life and her self.

While Nainaji's life resonate with the pattern of many women's lives, it also resonates with the lives of artistes, and reflects the breaks and crises that mark their lives. In her telling, these acquired for me the magnitude of metaphors. The most important of these are, I think, the metaphors of illness and of pilgrimage.

In the life of many artistes you will find the motif of a terrible illness that threatens the very source of their expression. This illness, while imposing a period of silence and withdrawal, is also the means by which the artiste makes contact with someone or something, to receive and discover a special gift, to become more than just a competent performer. In Nainaji's life marriage brought a rupture with the home of her childhood, and it brought with it a time of silence. However, this long period of silence in Nainaji's life made her sensitive to the music and lives of tawaifs. Widowhood brought her great sorrow and hardship, but also brought her back to music. And then just as things seemed to be proceeding smoothly, an illness, a total loss of voice. Yet, she was miraculously cured, and the cure brought with it a special gift, lifting her art above mere virtuosity, imbuing it with the gift of the elusive, magical taseer of music. The gift of taseer brought that special quality to her singing that surpassed the perfection that come from taleem and riyaz alone.

Then, there is the metaphor of pilgrimage. Learning music is a quest, a search for the secret of pure swara and for the essence of music. Every artiste has stories to tell of terrible hardships and sufferings endured—sleepless nights of non-stop riyaz, thrashings from a hard-to-satisfy guru, the giving up of friends, family life, foods one has enjoyed, pretty clothes. One holds up a bent finger, directs your gaze to a torn ear. Another recalls tying his hair to a tree to prevent himself from dozing as he practised. Yet another tells of singing every morning for five hours before her father would allow her to eat. Others leave homes and families searching for the secret heart of music.

As with pilgrimage, suffering is a marker of the journey. To complain, to turn back, is to condemn oneself eternally because it means denying the truth about oneself. Having embarked on the journey, the pilgrim goes on, relentlessly. Sometimes, as in Nainaji's own case, suffering directs the pilgrim's unconscious footsteps. What was only dimly perceived, sometimes even unseen, is now perceived with an overpowering clarity. Suffering tears the obscuring veil, allowing the artiste to perceive his or her true destiny.

Religion was important in Nainaji's life. Like her grandfather, she was a believer in the oneness of all religions. In her own way she tried to find a universal, syncretic ideology, and to communicate it. Her own journey led her to Sufism and Raaz Piya.

But there is another sense in which religion is important. Though Nainaji would often laugh and say that one cannot sing thumri too seriously as if it were a bhajan—it has to be erotic—music is itself a spiritual quest. Drawing from the Bhagavata Purana, Nainaji, believed that in Kali Yuga, artistes, like women and shudras are specially privileged—the artiste needs only to sing or dance to please God. At the same time, she was not bound by a single faith. Nainaji saw herself as neither Hindu nor Muslim but as all, or none of these. On the one hand, she could, and did, worship with full faith in temples, dargahs, churches and gurdwaras; on the other, these external forms seemed unimportant. It was the essence of religion that she sought, and to her, the essence was to be found in music. She saw herself as belonging to the musical family, and this family was simultaneously a religious community. With extraordinary symmetry, there was the other sense of belonging—the belonging to the religious family of the spiritual guru (the pir) and his disciples—but again, this spiritual family was simultaneously a family involved in music.

In the transformations that music effects, the artiste ceases to be male or female. Using the female narrative voice, using a form that privileges a woman's emotions, steeped in the culturally shared notions of madhurya bhakti and shringar rasa, I think singing thumri redefines gendered identities. Femininity is redefined in the subversive performative style of thumri gayaki. In the singing of thumri, femininity and masculinity are no more posed against each other; instead there seems to be a blurring of identities, the possibility of an androgynous selfhood. Femininity is not seen in terms of women's socially approved roles, but as shringar—true beauty, true passion, and the capacity to know one's self and one's perfection through the play of dualities, the pain of contradictions and the ephemeral joys of the world of texture, sound and colour—the world of rasa and raas.

So that for me, a woman singing this music that was once sung by courtesans, thumri becomes a mirror to see myself as human, as both wracked and delighted by the ever-changing seasons of emotion, as a woman living in my historical moment in this socio-cultural milieu, but also, as changeless, serene—beyond time and location—as whole, indivisible, one.

It is this new self that a singer, a woman like Nainaji, lives out in music. It is a self that is different, that stands apart from ordinary people, from the preoccupations and priorities of ordinary lives. The singer is neither Hindu nor Muslim, neither male nor female, neither old nor young. The artiste's body and being are liminal, magical, transformative.

It seems that there are primarily two ways of understanding lives. There is the life that is impelled forward by a sense of telos, a goal-oriented, purposeful life, the arrow that flies out to meet a target. And there is the other kind of life typified by the eternal round of the life cycle. Possibly, in patriarchal societies it is easier to see the lives of men as fitting the former pattern. In the latter pattern, both continuities and discontinuities flow from the events of the life cycle, and possibly, in traditional societies, this form is experienced more by women.

I think of my beloved guru and wonder if a life like Nainaji's is not somehow different. Two things come to my mind. The first—that perhaps for the woman artiste life's pattern is more in the nature of a spiral, that beautiful form of seashell and coiled serpent, a form that, like the avartan of a tala, is simultaneously cyclical and progressive. The second—I see how Nainaji has treated life creatively, improvising, spinning out new meanings, finding and extending space in the givens of the narrative of her life, so that what exists and what is inevitable becomes eternally new, fertile, a source of wonder and joy. And so, it has been possible for her to live gracefully and beautifully. It seems to me that she has learnt how to make bandhan into bandish. Bandhan is bondage, but bandish is that musical piece that, set and fixed, is yet not a foreclosed narrative. The singer is free to wander, to play, even transgress the vast landscape of the song, but always return to the mukhra and the sam. The bandish is fully mapped, the raga is fixed, so is the tala and the sahitya. But the meaning of what is sung is not fixed, ever, but changes with every rendering.

In such a situation, deprivation, sorrow and hardship are, as much as are pleasurable experiences, places to pause and contemplate; good fortune and bad are both benedictions. Life then is neither a bondage to be endured or fought against, nor is it a goal to be achieved. It is a wonderful gift to and from oneself.

9

Moving On

Nainaji is no more. At the time she died it had felt as if the world had come to an end. Something had indeed come to an end. A whole phase of my life was over.

Her death left me feeling strangely orphaned. Yet it also made me aware that this too, the absence of the guru is important. It is part of the journey I had to make. I realized that her absence was as much her gift to me as her presence. It has meant delving deeper into whatever she had taught me, recalling and reliving everything, yet knowing very well that memory is a perfidious record.

Her absence has made me aware of having to journey on, to travel now on my own, seeking teachers along the way, but with the knowledge that I am, as we all are, totally alone.

My life with her was rich beyond belief. Every day brought new experiences, new moments of joy and pain, new understandings, new food for thought. She was a generous teacher, and each day I spent with her was filled with more bandishes than I could absorb. My life with her was woven around the bandishes she taught me, around improvisatory flights through the raga.

All that changed with her passing.

For a while after her passing, her home witnessed, as it

had during her lifetime, the steady tramp of footsteps. Many musicians, friends, patrons, relations poured in to pay their last respects and to offer their music to her memory.

Then the house in Kaka Nagar fell silent. Now someone else lives there, and I have never gone back to that space where I spent so many years with her.

I often wonder though, whether the house's new occupants have discovered the unknown Sufi's mazaar under the pipal tree in the garden. Does anyone light a lamp there on Monday nights as she had done for so many years? Do nasturtiums still grow there in winter? And does the kitchen garden at the back yield its tiny but delicious harvest of gobhi and hara dhania, mooli and palak? Does someone arrange roses in a silver vase in a simple yet elegantly furnished room? What pictures have replaced the miniature paintings on the walls of the house I knew? Does music still echo through the rooms? Does the sound of laughter?

Soon after Nainaji's passing, her daughter, Rena Singh, set up the Naina Devi Foundation in her memory. For a few years the Foundation organized an annual festival of music and dance. Though for some time now these have not taken place, the Foundation has continued, silently, its work of supporting senior artistes through a health insurance scheme. Nainaji would have appreciated that. The cause of aging and infirm artistes was something she herself had taken up, informally all her life.

During her lifetime Nainaji had often bemoaned the fact that few singers opted to focus exclusively on thumri. While many artistes learned thumri, most of them sang it to round off a performance. Few at that time cared (or dared) to devote an entire performance to thumri. That has changed. There are today more young students aspiring to

learn thumri, there are many young performers who choose
to specialize in this form. No longer is thumri considered a
slightly suspect form, grudgingly accepted as a 'light classical'
piece. Most recently Vinod Kapur, in addition to the series
of monthly baithaks he organises, has initiated a programme
to discover and sponser young singers of thumri. All this
would surely have gladdened her heart.

Different people remember and view her contribution in
different ways. There are some who remember the woman
called Nilina Ripjit Singh, who, sans tabla or sarangi, with
only her own harmonium accompanying her, spontaneously
sang what she had heard of the popular singers of the day.
As yet untutored, singing only to please herself and friends,
that woman was not yet the singer she later became. She
had not yet discovered and explored the extent of her gayaki
and range. Perhaps she had not yet discovered herself.
Others recall what she became by sheer perseverance—in
the face of tremendous odds—a woman called Naina Devi
who learned and perfected the subtle art of thumri gayaki.
She is remembered too for her adherence to the traditional
style of the 'classical' thumri, and for her vast and varied
repertoire of bandishes that she shared so generously with
her shagirds.

Who can forget the exquisite jhoola, one of her favourite
bandishes, that describes Sita swinging on the banks of the
Sarayu river. Clothed in silken garments, her snake-like plait
flying in the breeze, Sita swings to the rhythm of Nainaji's
voice. This piece is less folksy than most jhoola bandishes
that we hear. It has a slower pace, a sense of thehraav—the
calmness and repose that one would normally associate with
bol banao thumri. This jhoola also permits of a vast range
of improvisations—the jagah possible here make it almost a

'classical' piece. 'Ustadon ki cheez hai'—the composition of a master—is how connoisseurs have described it.

Another bandish that never fails to move one is her own compostion—the Maand thumri *'Nipat kapat sainyaan'*. In the voice of the uttama-khandita nayika, this thumri articulates the reproach of the woman deceived by her beloved. Nainaji's musical composition echoes the poetry's reproach in the sweep and fall of Maand's elongated notes. Nainaji's Maand brings the vastness of this desert melody into the intimate space of the mehfil.

Moujuddin Khan's composition, *'Savariya, kahe mare najariya'*, a dadra set in Pancham se Gara was another of her favourites. Dadras like *'More naina laage'* charmed us for their inbuilt layakari, play with rhythm, the missed beats and the hidden sam.

Along with this more 'classicized' repertoire, she was also one of the few 'modern' singers to have heard and learnt the traditional 'nathni' bandishes sung at the time of the nath-utarwai initiation ceremony of the tawaifs. In my memory, I never heard her sing these in public, though she would often recall them and share them with me, remembering too and describing hearing one of these from none other than her gurubhai Sunil Bose. Sometimes she would change the words, rework the theme slightly to make these compositions more acceptable to a contemporary audience. And sometimes, especially in her last days, she would remember the songs she had heard and sung as a young bride of the Kapurthala rajwada, recounting those days and those songs that did not form part of the more classicized repertoire for which she became justly famous.

Now I only hear her voice in the few commercial recordings she made (this was before the flood of music recordings made possible by cassette and CD technology) and the many informal recordings I was able to make of her teaching.

Despite her absence, I realize, my life has not ceased to be rich. Far from feeling depleted by her death, I realize now that I feel her presence at all times, at all moments. Memories arise, and I am able to see those moments in a different light now, perhaps with a greater depth of understanding than I could have been capable of then. For I am older now. I have lived a few more years, garnered a little more experience.

Sometimes I half wish that I could have been her shagird now, that I could experience her teaching from the perspective with which I now view both life and music. Then I realize the foolishness of this. People come into our lives at the time that is right for us both, when we are ready for them, and indeed when they are ready for us—when we have something to say to each other. Then they leave us when our journey together is over, when the debts we owe each other have been repaid. And perhaps, their leaving us is also their gift to us, a strangely harsh gift, yet no less precious. For the death of my guru implies the loss of the shade of her presence in this kadi dhoop ka safar that is the world. Yet it makes me aware that the presence of the guru is within me. Nainaji continues to be here, she is ever-present. It is a different presence though, and one that teaches me another important lesson. Her absent presence encourages me to understand that I now have to find my own path, and in finding it, find my own self. It gives me the world to traverse; it asks me to make my own journey, to find my own voice, to sing my own song.